❧ Vegetarian Balti Cooking

Mridula Baljekar

Illustrations by Ken Cox

Thorsons
An Imprint of HarperCollins*Publishers*

Thorsons
An Imprint of HarperCollins*Publishers*
77–85 Fulham Palace Road,
Hammersmith, London W6 8JB

1160 Battery Street,
San Francisco, California 94111–1213

Published by Thorsons 1995

1 3 5 7 9 10 8 6 4 2

© Mridula Baljekar 1995

Mridula Baljekar asserts the moral right to
be identified as the author of this work

A catalogue record for this book is available from the British Library

ISBN 0 7225 3137 0

Printed in Great Britain by Woolnough Bookbinding Ltd.

In memory of my grandmother
who inspired me as a child.

Acknowledgements

I wish to thank KT Achaya, author of *Indian Food – A Historical Companion* which has been invaluable in collecting information about food, cooking utensils and crops in the Indus Valley Civilization. The book has also been very helpful in providing material about Kashmir and its food.

I would also like to thank Kathleen Cox for her excellent travel book, Fodor's *The Himalayan Countries* which has given me a deep insight into the North West Frontier Province where Baltistan is situated.

The Reader's Digest *Library of Modern Knowledge* has been an excellent source of information in compiling some of the historical facts.

I am grateful to Major Manoj Pandey of the Indian Army for explaining in simple terms some of the points about Kashmir and its surrounding areas.

My thanks to the following Balti restaurants:

Planet Pappodum, Chelsea, London
Royal Naim, Birmingham
Sher Khan, Birmingham
Adil's Balti House, Birmingham
'I am the King of Balti', Birmingham

My thanks also to Dr Dhiraj Mahanta for escorting me to the above restaurants.

Many thanks to my husband for his help in proof-reading each recipe and acting as a computer help line!

Last, but not least, many thanks to my lovely daughters, Maneesha (13), and Sneha (9), for leaving me alone to get on with the book!

❧ Contents

❧ Introduction

Balti cuisine is currently hot news throughout Britain. Many of my friends and relations have often asked me 'What is Balti food?' 'Is there really a place called Baltistan?'

During the recent past, I had heard several people talking about Balti food but was not quite sure of its origin: we had never come across this term in India. I was, therefore, determined to find out its roots and embarked on extensive research into the subject.

To my amazement, I discovered that Balti cuisine was very similar to a technique which I have always known as 'karahi cooking'! It is an extremely popular method in Northern India, especially in the Himalayan states.

I also found that people had heard of a place called Baltistan but I was unable to locate it in any of the maps I had seen so far. Then one day, glancing through an old copy of the Reader's Digest World Atlas, I suddenly spotted Baltistan! It is a small region nestling in the triangle formed by three of the world's highest mountain ranges, just above Kashmir, in India. But what was the connection between karahi cooking and Baltistan?

After browsing through several books about the Northern

Territories, I found one that was particularly useful. This was Fodor's Travel Guide, entitled 'The Himalayan Countries'. Through the excellent details in this book I was finally able to establish the karahi-Balti link.

Basically, 'Balti' refers to the utensil and the technique used in this cuisine.

The early Baltistani settlers, believed to be nomads, arrived from Tibet and christened their new land 'Tibet-i-Khurd' or Little Tibet. They carried all their worldly possessions upon their backs. The karahi, resembling the Chinese wok, was one of them. This is still in use all over the Northern states. The cooking style used in Baltistan became known as 'Balti cuisine' in Pakistan. This is probably because Baltistan, though originally a part of pre-independent India, now belongs to Pakistan. In India this style is known as 'karahi cuisine'.

So how did Baltistan become a part of Pakistan?

When the British finally left India in 1947, they partitioned it into two countries: India and Pakistan. The Hindu Rajas (kings) and Muslim Nawabs (dukes), who held vast estates in Kashmir, were given the option of joining one or the other of the new young nations. The Raja of 'Jammu and Kashmir' hesitated, hoping he would be given independent status.

In the meantime, Pakistan, fearing Hindu domination of Kashmir, crossed the Indo-Pakistan border. The Raja of Kashmir at once decided to side with India, which sent in troops to defend the territory. Thus the first Indo-Pakistan war broke out; the United Nations intervened and drew a ceasefire line across the terrain. The bulk of the disputed territory of

Kashmir was awarded to India.

Pakistan retained the area north of the ceasefire line and called it FANA (Federally Administered Northern Areas). They divided the region into two: the western part was called Gilgit, the eastern part, formerly Tibet-i-Khurd, is Baltistan.

The location of Baltistan is described by some as the 'roof of the world'. It is situated in the triangular area formed by the Himalayas, the Karakoram and the Hindu Kush range of mountains. It is here that you will find Mt Godwin-Austin (known more popularly as K2), second only to Mt Everest at 8,660 metres (28,413 ft). This area also boasts the world's longest glaciers outside the polar regions. There is a shortage of oxygen in these high altitudes and because of the low atmospheric pressure, water boils at 70°C (21°F)!

Marco Polo supposedly passed through here between 1271 and 1275 on his way to China. He recorded that no living soul or birds or animals could survive there as the air was so cold. Firewood burned slowly and did not have the same bright glow as elsewhere.

There are over 100 summits that tower 7,000 metres (22,965 ft) and many rise to 8,000 metres (26,246 ft). Tons of silt, brought down from the upper reaches of the mountains, form massive sand dunes in rivers that cascade through ravines.

Lakes reflect the sun and vast fields are effective grazing grounds for sheep and yaks. Fish abound in the rivers and wildlife is everywhere. This is an area of rugged and, in some parts, almost inhospitable beauty.

A few thousand miles to the south-west, archaeologists

3

discovered evidence of the evolution of the world's third literate society. This is the famous Indus Valley Civilization, which lasted for about 1,000 years.

The Food

Balti food is basically a variation of Kashmiri cooking with the distinctive aroma of spices characteristic of this region. The flavours are diverse and delightful: they are derived from the influence of rich Mogul cuisine, light and aromatic Chinese dishes, and the slightly stronger, hotter flavours of tribal cooking. All of these incorporate the vital winter foods and spices which are essential in the extremely cold climate of these high altitudes.

The cooking technique has emphatic Chinese overtones, especially the process of 'stir-frying'. Overlaid on this is the influence of hundreds of years of Mogul, Persian, Hun and Arabic cultures and the evolution of the communal eating habits of the people. Eating straight out of the pan in which the food was cooked, was perfect for a nomadic lifestyle. The 'Balti' was placed on the centre of the table, and a massive naan accompanied the meal — the whole family breaking off little pieces to scoop up the curry; no cutlery, no crockery, only one pan to wash, and an economical use of firewood.

Although naan is the traditional accompaniment to Balti meals, rice is grown and eaten in the area. The foothills of the Himalayas produce the king of all long-grain rice. This is the exquisite basmati.

Wheat, maize and other grains are also grown in the area. A

wide range of fruits and vegetables grown in the summer are dried and stored for the long winter months. As meat is scarce during the winter months, Baltistanis eat more lentils, fruit and vegetables.

Balti in India

Balti, or karahi, cooking adds a whole new dimension to Indian cuisine. It is a very simple concept, with a humble origin, arising out of the basic necessity of mankind. In the early days none of the pots and pans that we have today were available. Archaeological findings in the Indus Valley sites near Baltistan reveal cooking pots and pans in shapes that are still used in India. These were made of either copper or cast iron. The karahi or Balti pan is one such item which is used extensively in Northern India. I grew up with karahi cooking; every family meal was cooked in a karahi.

In Assam, in the eastern foothills of the Himalayas, where I was born and brought up, I watched Pathans walking up and down our streets selling walnuts, almonds, cherries and precious stones. They carried their goods in cone-shaped cane baskets on their backs or round cane baskets on their head. The Pathans, originally from Israel, are tall, well-built and very good looking people; as young girls, we used to rush to the front verandah to catch a glimpse of these handsome men while our mothers, grandmothers and aunts bargained with them for the goods they had come to sell. They came through the Khyber Pass from Israel, first settling their home

5

in Afghanistan where they were converted to Islam and eventually taking Islam to Baltistan. More than half of them live in the North West Frontier Province (now in Pakistan) created by the British to guard their India against foreign invaders.

Pakistan is a meat-eating nation and Balti cuisine is therefore associated with meat. On the other side of the border, in India, however, vegetables play an important part in the daily diet of the majority of its population. I have watched my grandmother cook scrumptious vegetable dishes in the karahi, and my mother create wonderful lentil, bean and vegetable dishes as well as meat and poultry ones. My grandmother used wood to fuel the clay stoves and ovens. The cast iron karahi, combined with the earthiness of the clay oven and the aroma of the wood imparted a unique flavour to the food.

Balti Britain

The triangular layout in the Himalayan region seems to be replicated in the Midlands where it is known, coincidentally, as the Birmingham Balti Triangle! The three roads that form this triangle are Stratford Road, Ladypool Road and Moseley Road. One hundred plus Balti restaurants do thriving business here. The total number of Balti restaurants in the entire city and its suburbs is close to 300!

Having visited several of these restaurants and having had a taste of the food in most of them, I realised that an imaginative but simple twist to traditional Indian cooking, is

6

beginning to have an impact similar to that which tandoori food had when it first arrived in Britain.

In this book, I offer you a selection of wonderful vegetarian recipes, drawn on the memories of a childhood which was rich in culinary expertise. In later years, I have been fortunate enough to learn vegetarian cooking techniques from my mother-in-law who has been a vegetarian all her life.

The recipes are easy to follow: the majority are traditional but some are innovative. I have extended the range by using the huge variety of ingredients available to us, here in the West.

I hope you enjoy cooking them and sharing the wonderful results with your family and friends.

The Balti Kitchen

The Balti Pan

An authentic cooking pan can be bought from most Asian grocers, who also sell other cooking utensils. A wok, however, will be perfectly adequate. There are several companies in Birmingham who sell Balti pans and they will usually provide a mail order service.

Preparing a Balti Pan before Cooking

A Balti, wok or karahi needs to be 'seasoned' before being used for the first time. Firstly, it should be washed in hot, soapy water and rinsed several times. Next, place the pan over high heat and allow all the water to dry completely. Then add two to three tablespoons of any cooking oil and heat until the oil is smoking. Remove the pan from the heat and swirl it around so that a thin film of oil covers the entire inner surface. Allow to cool, pour off the oil and wipe the pan dry with kitchen paper. You have now started the process of a build-up of a protective film which will be enhanced by repeated use of the pan, rendering it almost non-stick.

Cleaning a Balti Pan

Your pan will give you years of successful service if you follow a few basic cleaning and storing guidelines.

As mentioned above, 'seasoning' will help to create a protective film which, with repeated use and aftercare, will become a natural non-stick surface.

The best way to clean a pan is with hot soapy water. *Do not* use abrasive powder or harsh creams, and *never* use a metal or a sharp scouring pad. There are non-scratch scouring pads available which are meant for non-stick pots and pans. These are ideal. You can also use a wok cleaner available from Chinese supermarkets.

After you have washed the pan, dry it thoroughly, then rub a little oil on the entire inner surface before storing it. Do this each time you wash the pan. You will eventually end up with a blackened pan by which time you will have become an expert at Balti cooking! (Incidentally, a blackened pan is said to be an indication of a good cook!)

It is a good idea to have at least three different sizes of pans: large, medium and small. Very small karahis, which are meant for serving only, are also available. I prefer to take my cooking pan straight to the table — it's much more fun!

Electrical Tools

Unlike the ancient nomads, we have the benefit of electrical gadgets in our kitchen: make them work for you!

Make onion, ginger and garlic purée in a blender or food processor and store each one in small quantities. I keep these in a set of airtight containers in the fridge for frequent use. Use 1½ teaspoons of puréed garlic when a recipe calls for 3–4 cloves of garlic. Similarly, use 1½ teaspoons of puréed root ginger for a 2.5cm/1 inch cube. A little more or less garlic or ginger will not have a dramatic effect on your dishes.

Of course you can buy ginger and garlic purée ready to use, but they will not have the wonderful flavour which you get by making your own.

I also store a good quantity in small containers in the freezer.

You can chop fresh coriander in the food processor and freeze it in a freezer container. Break off small portions and use as required. Fresh green chillies can be frozen and used straight from the freezer too. They will keep better if you freeze them with the stalks intact.

A coffee mill is essential for grinding dry spices.

Using the Pressure Cooker

If you have a pressure cooker, use it to cook lentils, dried beans and peas quickly and efficiently. These can be frozen and used for your Balti dishes as and when required.

Freezing Cooked Food

A majority of the dishes in this book will freeze successfully, as long as you are careful about what and how you freeze.

Vegetables such as potatoes (except when mashed), and to a certain extent aubergine, do not freeze very well. Most other vegetables will freeze better if they are absolutely fresh when used.

All peas, beans and lentil dishes are excellent for freezing. Cooked rice dishes and all breads also freeze very well.

When cooking for the freezer, it is wise to undercook the vegetables slightly. Cool the dish quickly and chill before freezing. Spicy dishes taste even better when defrosted and reheated.

Always thaw the dish thoroughly before reheating. Do not panic if you find that your thawed dish has a lot of water content. This is because a certain amount of separation takes place when a dish is thawed. Do not attempt to drain it off, the vegetables will absorb all the water back into themselves during reheating.

When the dish is thawed and reheated, you may find that you need to adjust the salt and garam masala.

Here is a simple tip you can follow to give your defrosted dish an absolutely fresh appearance and flavour.

Heat about 2 teaspoons of cooking oil or ghee in a karahi. Add ¼–½ teaspoon garam masala, depending on the amount of food you have, and a pinch of salt. Add the thawed dish and stir-fry until heated thoroughly adding a little warm water if it becomes too dry. Stir in about 1 tablespoon of chopped fresh coriander leaves.

The dish will taste as fresh as if you have just cooked it!

Storing Balti Dishes in the Fridge

The characteristic feature of Balti food is its freshness. However, I do not advocate throwing away the leftovers.

Make sure the food is cold and put in an airtight container before storing in the fridge. Dishes containing acid ingredients like tomatoes, tomato purée and lemon juice will preserve the food for 48 hours, or longer, in perfect condition. Other dishes will keep well, though some vegetables may turn softer and the dish may look paler.

Follow the tips I have given for 'freshening up' frozen dishes.

How to Serve a Balti Meal

You can have enormous childlike fun by serving your Balti meal in the traditional way. Take your Balti pan straight to the table, and serve it with as big a naan as you can comfortably fit into your oven. Have two or three naan if you have a large gathering.

Remember, you can also serve rice with your Balti meals and add all the chutneys, relishes and pappodums too.

You can also buy mini Balti serving dishes, as previously mentioned. These are made of steel and they can be used for salads and raitas. For small parties, you can use these to serve your Balti dishes.

Cutlery is not used for Balti food; you simply break off small pieces of naan and scoop up the curries with them. Whether you want to eat the traditional way or with knives and forks, it is really for you to decide. If you have rice on the menu, you will probably find it easier to eat with a fork or spoon.

How to Store Spices and Prolong their Shelf Life

All the traditional Indian spices are used in Balti cooking. Whole spices have a much longer shelf life than ground. All spices, whole or ground, should be stored in airtight containers in a cool dark place. Ground spices lose their flavour very quickly even when they are stored properly.

The best way to preserve the flavour of spices is to heat them gently before storing. Simply preheat a heavy-based pan, add your chosen spice and stir until it releases its aroma. As soon as this happens, remove the pan from the heat and spread the spice on a large plate or tray.

Allow to cool thoroughly before storing in an airtight

container. Ground spices treated this way will keep fresh for up to 12 months – whole spices even longer.

If you wish to buy whole spices and grind them yourself (this will always give you the best results) heat them gently as above, then cool and grind them. This heating not only enhances their flavour, but will also make them easier to grind.

Techniques of Preparing and Cooking Spices

Spices for Balti or karahi cooking are traditionally pounded to a coarse finish rather than finely ground. This is in keeping with the ancient tradition started by the Indus Valley Civilization where most of the grinding operations were done on brick platforms using wooden pestles.

But if your palate is not used to coarse spices, it can be rather unpleasant. I prefer to use the finely ground spices generally used in all Indian cooking.

For cooking the spices, always start on a medium or medium-to-high heat: *never* very high. For best results preheat your Balti pan or karahi briefly before adding oil. Do not allow the oil to over-heat as the spices will burn quickly imparting an unpleasant, slightly bitter flavour to the dish.

Using Salt

In Indian cooking, salt is used more as a spice rather than a seasoning agent. The quantity of salt used may appear

13

excessive to the Western cook, but a certain minimum amount of salt is required to create a more balanced flavour of the spices. Without this, the dishes do not have the same authentic flavour. However, it is really up to you to decide how much salt you would like to use.

Cooking and Serving Rice

Cooking rice to perfection is quite easy if you follow a few simple steps.

Before cooking: rice has quite a large amount of milling starch which you need to remove first. To do this, always wash the rice in several changes of water and soak it for 30 minutes then drain well. This process will not only remove much of the starch but will also enable the rice to absorb the water more easily during cooking giving you perfectly fluffy, dry and separate grains.

During cooking: once you have put the lid on *never* be tempted to look at the rice. Leave it to cook for the specified time without lifting the lid or stirring it.

After cooking: remove the pan from the heat as soon as the rice is ready and keep it undisturbed for at least 10 minutes. Freshly cooked rice is rather fragile and allowing it to rest is very important. Fork through the rice and use a flat plastic or metal spoon to serve. Wooden ones tend to squash the grains.

❄ Special Ingredients

The following is a list of the most commonly used ingredients in Indian and Pakistani cooking. You will also find hints about storing spices which require special care and attention.

Atta or chapatti flour: this is a very fine wholewheat flour used to make all Indian unleavened bread. It is rich in dietary fibre because unlike other wholemeal flour, atta is produced by grinding the whole wheat kernel to a very fine powder.

Ajowan or carum: ajowan is native to India and looks rather like a celery seed. It is related to caraway and cumin though in flavour it is more akin to thyme. All Indian grocers stock ajowan and the seeds will keep for a number of years if stored in an airtight container. Only tiny amounts are used in pulse dishes and fried snacks. Ajowan helps to prevent wind.

Bay leaf (tej patta): bay leaves used in Indian cooking are obtained from the cassia tree. They are quite different from Western bay leaves, which come from the sweet bay laurel. Indian bay leaves are rarely available in the West; standard bay leaves have become a popular substitute.

Black peppercorns (kali mirchi): fresh green berries are dried in the sun to obtain black pepper. The green berries come from the pepper vine native to the monsoon forests of South West India. Whole peppercorns will keep well in an airtight jar while ground black pepper loses the wonderful aromatic flavour very quickly. It is best to store whole pepper in a pepper mill and grind it only when required. Pepper is believed to be a good remedy for flatulence.

Cardamom (elaichi): cardamom has been used in Indian cooking since ancient times. Southern India produces an abundance of cardamom from where it found its way to Europe through the Spice Route. There are two types of cardamom; the small green (choti elaichi) ones and the big dark brown (badi elaichi). In the West we also see a third variety. These are obtained by blanching the small green cardamom, and they have a milder flavour. Whole cardamom pods are used to flavour rice and different types of sauces. Ground cardamom, used in many desserts and drinks, can be bought from most Asian stores. It is best to grind small quantities at home using a coffee mill. Prolonged storage dries out the essential natural oils which destroys the flavour.

Cassia and cinnamon: cassia, used as cinnamon in Indian cooking, is one of the oldest spices. It is the dried bark of a tropical plant of the same name. Cinnamon is obtained from the dried bark of a tropical plant related to the laurel family. Cinnamon stick is indigenous to Sri Lanka which has complete monopoly. Cassia, on the other hand, grows all over the tropical countries. They produce similar flavours, but cinnamon is sweeter and more mellow.

Chillies (mirchi): it is difficult to judge the strength of chillies as different shapes and sizes will produce varying degree of pungency. Generally, the small thin ones are hot and the large fleshy ones tend to be milder. Most of the heat comes from the seeds and to have a gentle kick without too much heat it is best to remove them. One way to do this is to slit the chilli lengthwise into half and scrape the seeds away under running water. Use a small knife for this. Another way is to hold the chilli between your palms and roll it for a few seconds. This will loosen the seeds. You can then slit the chilli without cutting it through and simply shake out the seeds. Two types of chillies are normally used in Indian cooking:

Fresh green chillies (hari mirchi): the long slim fresh green Indian chillies are sold in Indian stores. Similar looking ones are sometimes sold in local greengrocers but these are usually from the Canary Islands and tend to be much milder than the Indian chillies.

Jalapeño and serrano chillies: from Mexico, these chillies are more easily available from supermarkets. Although these are not ideal for Indian cooking, they can be used when a recipe calls for fresh green chillies to be chopped or ground with other ingredients. When they are intended to be left whole, the long Indian variety look more attractive.

Dried red chillies (lal mirchi): when green chillies are ripe, their colour changes to a rich red. These are then dried to obtain dried red chillies. One cannot be substituted for the other as the flavour, when the chilli is dried, changes completely. The dried red 'Bird's eye' chillies which are small and pointed, are extremely hot and these are normally used whole to flavour the cooking oil. Long slim ones are much weaker and are used ground with other spices. Dried red chillies are ground to a fine powder to make chilli powder. Crushed dried chillies are obtained by grinding dried red chillies to a medium-coarse texture.

Cloves (lavang): cloves are unopened dried buds of a Southern Asian evergreen tree. They have a strong distinctive flavour and are used both whole and ground. In India cloves are used as a breath freshener, and clove oil is used to remedy toothache.

Coconut (nariyal): coconut palms grow in abundance in Southern India. Fresh coconut is used in both sweet and savoury dishes. In the West, convenient alternatives are desiccated coconut, creamed coconut and coconut milk powder. The use of coconut, however, is not common in Balti cooking.

Coriander, fresh (hara dhaniya): a much used herb in Indian cooking, especially in Balti cooking, the fresh leaves of the coriander plant are used for flavouring as well as garnishing. They also form the basis of many chutneys and pastes. The fruit produced by the mature coriander plant is the seed which is used as a spice, and from which fresh coriander is grown.

Coriander, seeds (dhaniya): this is one of the most important ingredients in Indian cooking. The sweet mellow flavour blends very well with vegetables.

Cumin seeds (jeera): like many spices cumin can be used either whole or ground. It is powerfully pungent and the whole seeds are used to flavour the oil before the vegetables are cooked in it. A more rounded flavour is obtained if the seeds are roasted and then ground. Because of their strength, they need to be used in measured quantities. There are two varieties, black (kala jeera) and white (safed jeera). Each has its

18

own distinct flavour and one cannot be substituted for the other. Black cumin is sometimes confused with caraway.

Curry leaf (kari patta): grown extensively in the foothills of the Himalayas, these have quite an assertive flavour. Sold fresh and dried by Indian grocers, they are used to flavour vegetables and pulses. Dried curry leaves should be stored in an airtight jar and the fresh ones, which have a better flavour, can be frozen and used as required.

Dhanna-jeera powder: this is simply a mixture of coriander and cumin seeds which are ground together. The mix produces a different flavour from using ground coriander and cumin individually. This is because when the seeds in dhanna-jeera powder are mixed and ground together their natural oils combine at the same time. If you cannot get the mix, you can make your own by using 60 per cent coriander seeds and 40 per cent cumin seeds.

Dried fenugreek (Kasoori methi): a strong and aromatic herb characteristic of Balti cuisine. It is native to the Mediterranean region and is cultivated in India and Pakistan. Both the seeds and leaves (fresh and dried) are used in cooking, though in Balti cooking the dried leaves are used more commonly.

Fennel seeds (saunf): these greenish-yellow seeds, slightly bigger than cumin, have a taste similar to anise. They have been used in Indian cooking since ancient times. In India, fennel is used as a breath freshener. The seeds are also chewed to settle an upset stomach.

Garam masala: the main ingredients of garam masala are cinnamon or cassia, cardamom, cloves and black pepper.

19

Other spices are added to these, according to preference. Balti garam masala is not available in the shops but it is easy to make your own (see the recipe on pages 28–9).

Garlic (lasoon): fresh garlic is indispensable to Indian cooking. Dried flakes, powder and garlic salt cannot create the same authentic flavour. Garlic is always used crushed or puréed as these two methods produce more flavour. Garlic is beneficial in reducing the level of cholesterol in the blood and its antiseptic properties aid the digestive system.

Ghee (clarified butter): ghee has a rich and distinctive flavour and is used liberally in Mogul food. There are two types of ghee, pure butterfat ghee and vegetable ghee. Butterfat ghee is made from unsalted butter and vegetable ghee from vegetable shortening. Ghee can be heated to a high temperature without burning. Both types of ghee are available from Indian stores and vegetable ghee is sold by some supermarkets. It is simple to make your own ghee. Melt unsalted butter over low heat and allow it to bubble gently. At this stage, you will hear a gentle splattering which is the moisture in the butter being driven off. After a while, the splattering will stop, indicating that most of the moisture has evaporated. Continue to heat the butter until the liquid is a clear golden colour and you can see the sediment (milk solids) at the bottom of the pan. This process can take up to 45 minutes depending on the quantity of butter you are using. Once the liquid and milk solids have separated, cool the butter slightly and strain it into a storage jar through a fine muslin. Ghee can be stored at room temperature. Vegetable ghee can be made the same way using margarine made of vegetable oils.

Ginger (adrak): fresh root ginger which has a warm woody aroma, is vital to Indian cooking. Dried, powdered ginger cannot produce an authentic flavour. Ginger is believed to improve circulation of the blood and reduce acidity in the stomach.

Mint (pudina): mint is native to Mediterranean and Western Asian countries and is an essential ingredient in Balti cooking. It is easy to grow and also available in most super-markets. Dried mint, however, is a good substitute. Bottled mint sauce, which has a lovely fresh aroma, works very well in many recipes.

Mustard seeds (sarsoon or rai): these are an essential ingredient in vegetarian cooking. Out of the three types, black and brown mustard seeds are commonly used in Indian cooking, and lend a nutty flavour to a dish. White mustard seeds are reserved for making pickles, and the green leaves are used as a vegetable.

Nutmeg (jaiphal): the nutmeg plant is unique as it produces two fruits in one; nutmeg and mace (javitri). Nutmeg has a hard dark brown shell with a lacy covering. This covering is mace which is highly aromatic. It is removed from the nutmeg before being sold. The best way to buy nutmeg is whole. Pre-ground nutmeg loses the lovely aromatic flavour quickly. Special nutmeg graters are available with a compartment to store whole nutmegs.

Onion (pyaz): this is one of the oldest flavouring ingredients and rarely is any Indian cooking done without it. Brown, red and snow white onions are grown and used extensively; the use of shallots and spring onions is also quite common.

Onion seeds (kalonji): these tiny black seeds are not produced by the onion plant. They are referred to thus because they have a striking resemblance to the onion seeds. Kalonji, available from Indian stores, are used whole for flavouring vegetables and pickles and to flavour Indian breads.

Paneer: paneer is often referred to as 'cottage cheese' in India, but it is quite different from Western cottage cheese. The only Western cheese which resembles paneer in taste, is ricotta, but, ricotta cheese cannot withstand the cooking temperatures that paneer can. Paneer is made by separating the whey from the milk solids and is an excellent source of protein. It is available from Asian stores or you can make your own (see pages 30–31).

Paprika: Hungary and Spain produce a mild sweet strain of pepper. Dried and powdered, this is known as paprika. 'Deghi Mirchi', grown extensively in Kashmir is the main plant which is used for making Indian paprika. It is a mild chilli pepper which tints the dishes with a brilliant red colour without making them excessively hot.

Poppy seeds (khus khus): the opium poppy, grown mainly in the tropics, produces the best poppy seeds. There are two varieties, white and black, but only the white seeds are used in Indian recipes. They are either ground, or roasted and ground, and help to give a nutty flavour to most sauces while also acting as a thickening agent.

Rose water: a special edible rose is grown in many parts of the country. The petals are used for garnishing Moghul dishes. They can also be crushed to extract their essence. This is diluted to make rose water which is utilised in savoury and sweet dishes.

Saffron (kesar): the saffron crocus grows extensively in Kashmir. Close to 250,000 stamens of this crocus are needed to produce just 450g (1lb) of saffron. It is a highly concentrated ingredient and only minute quantities are required to flavour any dish.

Shahi jeera (royal cumin): this is different from the normal cumin, and is sometimes known as black cumin seeds. It is a rare variety and, in India, grows mainly in Kashmir. It is also more expensive but its delicate and distinctive flavour is well worth the extra expense. The seeds will keep well almost indefinitely if stored in airtight jars.

Sesame seeds (til): these pale creamy seeds, with a rich and nutty flavour are indigenous to India. They are the most important of all the oil seeds grown in the world and India is the largest exporter of sesame oil to the West. The seeds are sprinkled over naan before baking, and are also used in some sweets and vegetables. They are an effective thickening agent for sauces.

Tamarind (imli): resembling pea pods when tender, tamarind turns dark brown with a thin hard outer shell when ripe. Chocolate brown flesh is encased in the shell which needs to be seeded before use. The required quantity of the flesh is soaked in hot water, made into a pulp and used in several dishes. These days, life is made easier by the availability of ready-to-use concentrated tamarind pulp. Lentils, peas, vegetable and chutneys benefit from its distinctive tangy flavour.

Turmeric (haldi): fresh turmeric rhizomes are dried and ground to give a rich yellow powder. India produces the   23 largest amounts of turmeric. The quantity used in dishes has to be just right to prevent a bitter taste.

Vanilla: second only to saffron in terms of plant-to-shop costs, vanilla pods retain their flavour for years. They are usually stored embedded in sugar. The sugar, now with a strong vanilla flavour, can be used in desserts. Vanilla essence is an effective alternative.

Yogurt (dahi): made with fresh whole milk, yogurt in India is almost always home-made. A mild flavour combined with a creamy texture it is a very useful ingredient in many dishes.

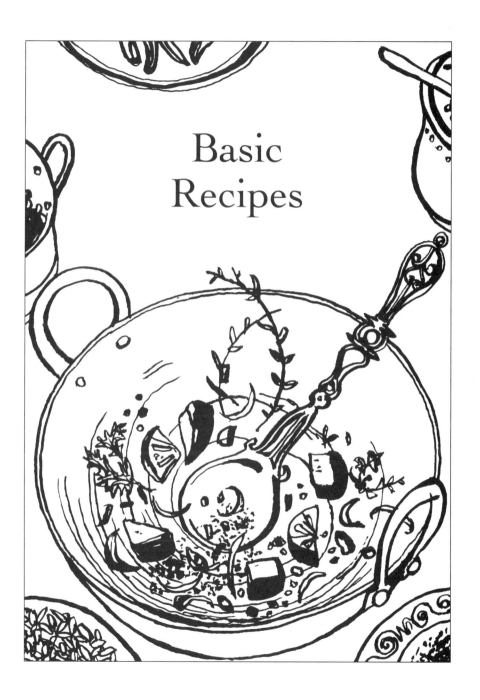

Basic
Recipes

Balti Base Sauce $\boxed{\text{V}}$

Makes 1.1 litres/2 pints

The advantage of using a 'base sauce' is one of convenience, especially if you want to create the flavours of restaurants at home. To meet their customers' demands quickly, the restaurants keep a base sauce ready for use.

Although it is not necessary to use a 'base sauce' for home cooking, should you wish to use one, then I suggest you prepare this in advance and store some in the fridge, for immediate use. Divide the remainder in quantities required by recipes and freeze them.

I was given this recipe by the Kashmiri chef at the Balti restaurant in Birmingham, called 'I am the King of Balti'!

450g/1lb onions, roughly chopped
25g/1oz root ginger, peeled and roughly chopped
40g/1½oz cloves garlic, peeled and roughly chopped
2 teaspoons ground turmeric
1 tablespoon ground coriander
1 ground tablespoon ground cumin
1½ teaspoons salt
1 tablespoon paprika

400g/14oz can tomatoes, including juice
600ml/1 pint water
1 tablespoon vegetable or corn oil

1. Put all ingredients together in a large saucepan over a high heat. Bring to the boil, reduce the heat to very low, then cover and simmer for 40–45 minutes.
2. Remove the saucepan from the heat and allow the contents to cool thoroughly, then purée until very smooth.
3. Store in a covered container in a fridge or freezer in required quantities.

Balti Garam Masala $\boxed{V}$

Makes 75g/3oz

The word 'garam' means 'heat' and 'masala' is a mixture of spices used to create a special flavour. Garam Masala is made by blending together a few specially chosen spices for which the recipe can vary from one region or one cook to another. However, the basic spices which are known to create body heat remain the same, ie cassia bark or cinnamon stick, cloves and cardamom. To these basic spices you can add other ingredients like black peppercorns, cumin and nutmeg. Balti Garam Masala, which is akin to Mogul Garam Masala, is made up of the basic winter spices to which a few other ingredients are added to create a flavour which characterizes the cooking of this region.

> 25g/1oz cassia bark or cinnamon sticks
> 25g/1oz whole green cardamom pods
> 15g/½oz whole cloves
> 8 bay leaves, broken up
> 2 teaspoons black peppercorns
> 3 whole nutmeg, crushed
> 3 teaspoons black cumin seeds

28

1. Preheat a karahi or wok over medium heat for 2–3 minutes. When hot, reduce the heat to low and add the cassia or cinnamon and cardamom pods. Stir and roast for 1 minute.

2. Add the cloves, bay leaves, peppercorns and nutmeg, stir and roast for 1½ minutes.

3. Remove the pan from heat and add the black cumin seeds. Your pan will still be hot enough to roast the seeds, stir and roast them for 1 minute.

4. Allow the spices to cool thoroughly, then grind in batches until fine in a coffee grinder. Mix the batches thoroughly and store in an airtight jar. This will remain fresh for 10–12 months.

Paneer

Makes 225g/8oz

Paneer is an Indian home-made cheese which is now being made commercially. You can buy paneer from Asian grocers and good supermarkets. It is a very versatile cheese and is full of all the goodness of protein and calcium. To the large vegetarian population of India, paneer provides as much protein as meat, poultry and fish. If you wish to make your own, you will be delighted to see from the recipe below, how easy it is to make. Unlike any other cheese, paneer needs no curing or maturing, which puts it in a class of its own.

2.6 litres/4½ pints full cream milk
125ml/¼ pint lemon juice

1. Heat the milk in a heavy-based saucepan, stirring frequently to prevent it sticking to the bottom of the pan.
2. When the milk begins to rise, add the lemon juice and let it boil until the whey is separated from the curdled milk. This will become obvious in a minute or two when the milk becomes watery and the cheese floats to the top.
3. Strain the curdled milk through a fine muslin and tie up

the ends loosely, leaving the cheese solids intact.

4. Hang the cloth in a cool place for 1 hour to allow all the water to drain off.

5. You can convert the paneer into a block by placing a weight on top. Hang the muslin for 5–10 minutes only, then roughly shape the Paneer into a block, leaving it in the cloth, and place a weight on top. Leave for 2–3 hours. Remove from the muslin and cut into cubes.

Starters and Appetizers

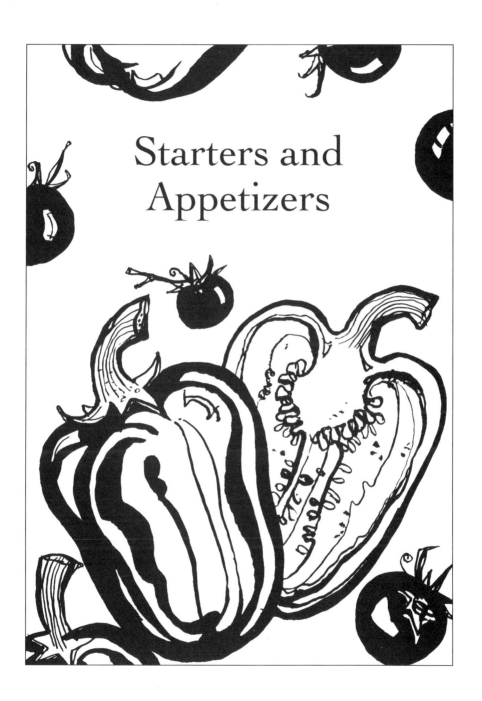

All Balti houses serve traditional tandoori dishes as starters. I felt I had to create some vegetarian starters so that you do not have to go without! Most of these are deep fried and the karahi or Balti pan is commonly used for this purpose in India and Pakistan.

Paneer Sashlik, which is grilled, is perhaps akin to the spit roasting method which was used by the Indus Valley settlers.

A mouth-watering choice of starters and appetizers are included in this chapter. These are also very versatile: you can serve some of them with drinks, or as side dishes; some can form a light meal. In every case, instructions are provided for different ways of serving them.

Shakahari Shamee Kabab

(Vegetarian Shamee Kabab)

Makes 12

Shamee Kabab is Mogul in origin and the Moguls, being Muslims, are basically meat eaters. I have created this vegetarian version using potato and paneer, the Indian cheese. Do make sure that you peel the potatoes after boiling, rather than before, to avoid any stickiness.

2 large slices white bread (about 100g/4oz)
375g/13oz potatoes, boiled, peeled and mashed
200g/7oz paneer, grated or mashed
1–2 green chillies, seeded and finely chopped
2–3 cloves garlic, peeled and crushed
½ teaspoon chilli powder (optional)
1 teaspoon salt or to taste
1½ teaspoons bottled mint sauce or 1 tablespoon finely
    chopped mint mixed with 1 tablespoon lime juice
15g/½oz finely chopped coriander leaves
1 small onion (about 100g/4oz), finely chopped or minced
25g/1oz plain flour, seasoned
1 large egg, beaten
Oil for shallow frying

1. Lay the slices of bread side by side on a large plate and pour over enough cold water to soak them for a few seconds. Hold the bread, one slice at a time, crumpled between your palms and squeeze out all the water. Put in a large mixing bowl.

2. Add the remaining ingredients except the flour, egg and oil. Using a potato masher, mash the ingredients until thoroughly blended together. Alternatively, put all the ingredients (except the onion, flour, egg and oil) in a food processor and blend until smooth. Add the onions and mix.

3. Divide the mixture into 2 equal parts and make 6 equal-sized balls from each. Flatten the balls into smooth round cakes.

4. Put enough oil in a frying pan to measure about 5mm/ ¼ inch depth and heat over medium heat. Dust each kabab in the seasoned flour, making sure it is fully coated. Dip the kababs in the beaten egg and fry until well browned on both sides. Drain on absorbent paper.

Preparation time: 25 minutes
Cooking time: 10–12 minutes
Serving ideas: Serve with a raita.

Suran Pakoras

(Spiced Yam Slices)

Serves 6 – 8

Suran or yam is also known as elephant yam and its use in Indian cooking dates back to the Aryan times. The Aryan civilization consisted of Nomadic tribes, some of whom settled in and around Baltistan.

If you have not cooked or eaten yam before, try this delicious spicy recipe. You can buy yam in good supermarkets and Asian stores.

> 900g/2lb yam
> 1 teaspoon salt or to taste
> 1 teaspoon ground turmeric
> 1–1½ teaspoons chilli powder
> 1 teaspoon ajowan (carum) seeds
> 25g/1oz besan (gram flour), sifted
> 15g/½oz ground rice
> Oil for deep frying

1. Peel the yam and cut into 5mm/¼ inch thick slices. As yam has rather thin ends and is quite thick in the middle, cut the bigger slices in half. Soak the slices in cold water

for 30 minutes, then drain but do not dry them.

2. Put the salt, turmeric, chilli powder, ajowan seeds, besan and ground rice in a large mixing bowl and mix well. Add the yam slices and mix until they are fully coated with the spiced besan.

3. Heat the oil for deep frying in a karahi or other suitable pan over medium-high heat. Fry the yam slices in batches in a single layer for 3–4 minutes or until they are crisp and golden brown. Drain on absorbent paper.

Preparation time: 15 minutes, plus 30 minutes to soak the yam
Cooking time: 12–15 minutes
*Serving idea*s: Serve with drinks or as a starter with Pudina aur Hara Dhaniya ki Chutney (pages 191–2).

Paneer Sashlik

(Indian Cheese Kababs)

$\boxed{V}$

Serves 6

Here is a wonderful vegetarian version of the well-known tandoori dish. Instead of lamb or chicken, you can use that versatile Indian cheese, paneer, to make these scrumptious kababs. If you cannot get or make paneer, use tofu instead.

For the marinade:

    2 tablespoons lime juice

    4 cloves garlic, peeled and crushed to a fine pulp

    2 teaspoons ground coriander

    1 teaspoon ground cumin

    ½ teaspoon ground turmeric

    ¼–½ teaspoon chilli powder

    ½ teaspoon Balti Garam Masala (pages 28–9)

    1 teaspoon salt or to taste

    3 tablespoons sunflower or corn oil

For the kababs:

    200g/7oz paneer, cut into 2.5cm/1 inch cubes

    75g/3oz red pepper, cut into 2.5cm/1 inch cubes

    75g/3oz green pepper, cut into 2.5cm/1 inch cubes

40

175g/6oz cauliflower florets, in 2.5cm/1 inch pieces

100g/4oz closed cup mushrooms, halved, or small whole
button mushrooms

150g/5oz red onions, peeled and cut to the same size as
the mushrooms

40g/1½oz butter, melted for basting

1. Mix together all the ingredients for the marinade in a small bowl.
2. Put the paneer, peppers, cauliflower, mushrooms and onions in a large mixing bowl. Pour the marinade over, then stir and mix thoroughly. Cover and leave to marinate for 3–4 hours, or overnight in the fridge. Remove from the fridge 30 minutes before cooking.
3. Preheat the grill to medium and line a grill pan with foil.
4. Thread the marinated paneer and the vegetables onto individual skewers, alternating them evenly. The onion pieces will separate when cut, just put together several pieces to make one chunky piece.
5. Place the skewered kababs on the prepared grill pan and brush over any remaining marinade. Place the tray about 10cm/4 inches below the grill and cook for 2–3 minutes. Brush with melted butter and cook for a further 2 minutes. Turn the skewers over and brush with the remaining melted butter, then cook for a further 4–5 minutes and remove.

Preparation time: 20–25 minutes, plus marinating
Cooking time: 10 minutes

41

Serving ideas: Serve with any naan accompanied by Ghia ka
   Raita (pages 186–7).

What to do with leftovers: Cook Kesari Chawal (pages 162–3),
   heat the paneer and vegetables by tossing them in a karahi
   over high heat for a few minutes. Mix with the rice to make
   a delicious cheese and vegetable pulao.

Gobi Pakoras

(Spiced Cauliflower Fritters)

Serves 4–6

The use of a karahi for deep frying is very popular all over India. The round-bottomed shape of the karahi makes it a very economical way to fry, and the heavy cast iron distributes and retains heat perfectly.

 1 cauliflower (about 375g/13oz when outer leaves
    removed)
 1 onion (about 175g/6oz), roughly chopped
 1cm/½ inch cube root ginger, peeled and roughly
    chopped
 4 cloves garlic, peeled and roughly chopped
 2 green chillies, seeded
 15g/½oz coriander leaves, including tender stalks,
    roughly chopped
 150ml/¼ pint water
 200g/7oz besan (gram flour), sifted
 75g/3oz ground rice
 1¼ teaspoons salt or to taste
 ½ teaspoon chilli powder (optional)
 ½ teaspoon ground turmeric

43

75ml/3 fl oz water
Oil for deep frying

1. Divide the cauliflower into 2.5cm/1 inch florets.
2. Put the onion, ginger, garlic, chillies and coriander leaves in a blender. Add the first measure of water and blend until smooth.
3. In a large mixing bowl, mix the besan, ground rice, salt, chilli powder (if used) and turmeric. Add the blended ingredients and remaining water and mix to a thick batter.
4. Heat the oil in a karahi or wok over a medium heat. The temperature of the oil should be about 160°C. Drop a tiny amount of the batter, about the size of a lemon pip, into the oil. If it surfaces immediately without browning, the oil is at the right temperature.
5. Increase the heat slightly and dip each cauliflower floret in the batter, making sure it is fully coated.
6. Fry as many pakoras as you can in a single layer without overcrowding the pan. Each batch will take 6–7 minutes to brown, turn them over once or twice. Drain on absorbent paper.

Preparation time: 15 minutes
Cooking time: 15–20 minutes
Serving ideas: Serve as a starter with Pudina aur Hara Dhaniya ki Chutney (pages 191–2) or Ghia ki Chutney (pages 184–5). They are wonderful with drinks too!
Suitable for freezing.
Variation: Use broccoli instead of cauliflower.

Tala hua Palak

(Batter-Fried Spinach Leaves)

Serves 4

This recipe has fond memories for me; my mother would pick large spinach leaves from the garden in the morning and serve them up for lunch, coated in a spicy batter and deep fried in the karahi. This was her subtle but very successful way of making some of us eat spinach!

> 12 large spinach leaves
> 90g/3oz besan (gram flour)
> 40g/1½oz ground rice
> ½ teaspoon ground turmeric
> ½ teaspoon chilli powder
> 1 teaspoon cumin seeds
> 1 teaspoon onion seeds (kalonji)
> ½ teaspoon salt or to taste
> 175ml/6 fl oz water
> Oil for deep frying

1. Wash the spinach leaves carefully without damaging them. Keep a 2.5cm/1 inch stem on each leaf. Dry thoroughly on absorbent paper.
2. Sift the besan into a large mixing bowl and add the

45

remaining ingredients except the water and oil. Mix the dry ingredients well, then gradually add water, mixing until you have a thick batter.

3. Heat the oil in a karahi or wok over medium-high heat. To check that the oil is at the right temperature, drop a tiny piece of the batter in the hot oil. If it surfaces immediately without browning, then the temperature is just right. If you have a thermometer, make sure that the oil is at least 180°C.

4. Hold each leaf by its stem and dip it in the batter, making sure it is fully coated. The stem should also be coated with the batter. Fry 2–3 leaves at a time, depending on the size of your karahi or wok. Cook until golden brown and crisp, this will only take 1–1½ minutes per batch. Drain on absorbent paper and serve immediately.

Preparation time: 15 minutes

Cooking time: 6–8 minutes

Serving ideas: Serve as a starter with Pudina aur Hara Dhaniya ki Chutney (pages 191–2).

Not suitable for freezing.

Palak Pakoras

(Deep Fried Spinach Balls)

$\boxed{\text{V}}$

Makes 24

I am always surprised when I come across people who dismiss spinach as uninteresting and tasteless. For me, spinach is one of the most wonderful vegetables, offering complete flexibility in the way it can be cooked. Even if you are generally not interested in spinach, just try this recipe once, you'll love it! For deep fried snacks such as pakoras and bhajiyas which are coated with besan, the temperature of the oil is very important. You need to fry them gently to ensure that the inside cooks well and the outside browns gradually giving it a crisp texture.

155g/5oz besan (gram flour)
60g/2oz ground rice
1 teaspoon salt or to taste
¼–½ teaspoon chilli powder (optional)
1 teaspoon ground cumin
2 teaspoons ground coriander
1 teaspoon ground turmeric
1 teaspoon fennel seeds
1–2 green chillies, seeded and finely chopped
150g/5oz spinach leaves, finely chopped

47

150g/5oz onions, chopped
150ml/¼ pint water
Oil for deep frying

1. Sift the besan into a large mixing bowl and add the remaining ingredients except the water and oil.
2. Mix together, then gradually add the water until you have a thick paste-like consistency. Make 24 walnut-sized balls, to make this easier, divide the mixture into 4 equal parts and make 6 balls from each part.
3. Heat the oil in a karahi or wok over medium heat. Check the temperature with a thermometer, if you have one, and ensure that it is at 160°C–170°C. If you do not have a thermometer, take a tiny amount (about the size of a pea) of the paste, without the vegetables, and drop it in the oil. If it surfaces immediately without browning, then the temperature is just right.
4. Fry the pakoras in a single layer in batches for 8–10 minutes, turning them over occasionally. Drain on absorbent paper.

Preparation time: 15–20 minutes
Cooking time: 20–25 minutes
Serving ideas: Serve as a starter with Ghia ki Chutney (pages 184–5). They are lovely with drinks too.
Suitable for freezing. Thaw and reheat under a preheated medium grill for 5–6 minutes, turning over half way through. Place the grill 15–25cm/6–8 inches away from heat.
Variation: Use methi leaves (fenugreek) instead of spinach.

Aloo Chaat

(Potato Relish)

Serves 4–6

Aloo Chaat is a famous North Indian appetizer. It is eaten cold and has a tangy, slightly hot flavour. Served sprinkled with Delhi or Bombay Mix, it makes a mouth-watering snack. Traditionally black salt is used, which is beneficial to the digestive system. I have, however, used ordinary cooking salt here. The tangy flavour comes from tamarind which is available in Asian shops. If you cannot get it use lemon juice, but the flavour will be different.

> 700g/1½lb old potatoes
> 2 tablespoons chopped coriander leaves
> 2 tablespoons mint leaves or 1 teaspoon bottled
> mint sauce
> 1 green chilli, seeded and chopped
> ¼–½ teaspoon chilli powder (optional)
> 1 teaspoon salt or to taste
> 1¼ teaspoons tamarind concentrate or 2 tablespoons
> lemon juice
> 2 tablespoons water
> 1 small red onion, finely chopped

To garnish:
    Bombay or Delhi Mix

1. Boil the potatoes in their skins, drain and cool thoroughly. Peel and dice into 1cm/½ inch pieces.
2. Put the remaining ingredients, except the onion, in a blender and blend until smooth. Pour this mixture over the potatoes and add the onion. Mix thoroughly.
3. Put into individual serving dishes and top with Bombay or Delhi Mix.

Preparation time: 20 minutes
Cooking time: 25–30 minutes

Shakurkandi Pakoras

V

(Sweet Potato Fritters)

Serves 4—6

Sweet potatoes are available in most Asian stores as well as good supermarkets. They can be peeled just like ordinary potatoes. Cooked in a spicy batter they produce a wonderful contrast of flavours and textures. The batter is made of besan which is also known as gram flour or chick pea flour. You can buy it from Indian grocers, good supermarkets and health food shops. The temperature of the oil is crucial in frying pakoras successfully. Too low a temperature will result in soggy pakoras. If the temperature is too high, it will brown quickly leaving the inside raw.

> 450g/1lb sweet potatoes
> 175g/6oz besan (gram flour)
> 75g/3oz ground rice
> 1 teaspoon salt or to taste
> 1 teaspoon ajowan (carum) seeds
> 1 teaspoon crushed dried chillies
> 1 teaspoon ground turmeric
> 1 tablespoon ground cumin
> 15g/½oz fresh coriander leaves, including

51

tender stalks, finely chopped
300ml/½ pint water
Oil for deep frying

1. Peel the sweet potatoes. Working from both ends, cut as many 5mm/¼ inch thick slices as possible. When the diameter of the slices gets bigger, cut the potato into half, lengthwise, and slice each half as before. Cut exceptionally large slices into quarters. You will have a few uneven shapes and sizes because of the varied sizes that sweet potatoes come in. Soak the sliced potatoes in salted water for 15 minutes, then drain and rinse.

2. Sift the besan into a medium-sized mixing bowl. Add the remaining ingredients except the coriander, water and oil. Mix thoroughly with a wooden spoon, then add the coriander and gradually add the water while you continue to mix. Make sure the batter is smooth. When all the water is added, you should have a smooth, thick batter.

3. Heat oil in a karahi, wok or other deep frying pan over medium heat. If you have a thermometer, check that the temperature of oil is 160°C–170°C. If you do not have a thermometer, drop a small portion (about the size of a pea) of the batter in the oil. If it floats to the surface straightaway without browning, then the temperature is right.

4. Dip each slice of potato in the batter making sure it is fully coated, and shake off any excess batter back into the bowl. Fry as many slices as you can manage in a single layer without overcrowding the pan. Cook until evenly

browned on both sides, turning over at least twice. Each batch
will take 5–6 minutes. Drain on absorbent paper.

Preparation time: 20 minutes
Cooking time: 20–25 minutes
Serving ideas: Serve with a relish as a starter or with drinks.
    Alternatively, serve as a side dish with any Balti curry.

Vegetables

Fresh vegetables are important to us whether we are vegetarian or not. They provide essential vitamins and minerals, and cooking them the Indian way further enhances their natural values.

For example, garlic reduces the level of cholesterol in the blood and has antiseptic properties which aid the digestive system. Ginger is beneficial in reducing acidity in the stomach.

From the wide selection of recipes in this chapter, you will see how wonderful and interesting vegetables can be. Do try the unusual ones too; clear instructions for cooking and preparing have been given for all of them.

Paneer Kofta Makhani

(Cheese Balls in a Spicy Butter Sauce)

Serves 4

This vegetarian version is just as delicious as the original meat kofta recipe. Paneer is packed with essential nutrients, to the vast majority of the Indian population it provides as much protein as meat and poultry.

The little fried koftas, without the sauce, are delicious served as a starter with an accompanying relish.

For the koftas:

225g/8oz paneer
2–3 cloves garlic, peeled and roughly chopped
1 green chilli, seeded and chopped
15g/½oz coriander leaves, including tender stalks, roughly chopped
½ teaspoon bottled mint sauce
1 teaspoon Balti Garam Masala (pages 28–9)
½ teaspoon salt or to taste
1 tablespoon milk
15g/½oz plain flour
Oil for shallow frying

For the makhani sauce:

    2 tablespoons sunflower or soya oil

    2 x 5cm/2 inch cassia bark or cinnamon sticks

    4 green cardamom pods, split open the top

    4 cloves garlic, peeled and crushed

    1cm/½ inch cube root ginger, peeled and finely grated

    1 small onion (about 100g/4oz), finely chopped

    2 teaspoons ground coriander

    1 teaspoon ground cumin

    ½ teaspoon ground turmeric

    ¼–½ teaspoon chilli powder

    2 tablespoons tomato purée

    65g/2½oz butter

    ½ teaspoon salt or to taste

    150ml/¼ pint passata or sieved canned tomatoes

    150ml/¼ pint single cream

    3–4 green chillies (long slim variety)

    ½ teaspoon Balti Garam Masala (pages 28–9)

    2 tablespoons chopped coriander leaves

1. Blend all the ingredients for the koftas, except the flour and oil, in a food processor. If you have home made paneer your mix will be very smooth. The ready-made paneer mix will be slightly coarse, but this will not affect the flavour.

2. Make 20 equal-sized balls from the mixture. This is easier to do if you divide the mixture into 4 equal parts and make 5 balls (koftas) from each. Compress them into neat, tight balls, making them as smooth as possible

59

without any surface cracks. Coat in the flour.

3. Preheat a karahi, wok or a heavy-based frying pan with a non-stick surface over a medium heat. Add enough oil for shallow frying and fry the koftas in batches until brown all over. Turn and move them around in the pan frequently to ensure even browning. Drain on absorbent paper and keep hot.

To make the sauce:

4. Preheat a karahi or wok over medium heat for 1–2 minutes, then add the oil. When hot but not smoking, add the cassia or cinnamon and cardamom pods, and allow to sizzle for 15–20 seconds.

5. Add the garlic and ginger and stir-fry for 30 seconds. Add the onion and stir-fry for 4–5 minutes or until the onion is just soft. Add the coriander and cumin, stir-fry for 30 seconds, then add the turmeric, chilli powder and tomato purée. Stir-fry for 1 minute.

6. Add the butter, salt, passata or sieved tomatoes, and simmer for 2–3 minutes. Stir in the cream, chillies and garam masala, and simmer for 5 minutes. Stir in the coriander leaves and remove from the heat.

7. Pour the hot sauce over the koftas and serve.

Preparation time: 35–40 minutes
Cooking time: 20 minutes
Serving ideas: Serve with Kesari Chawal (pages 162–3) or Soda Naan (pages 178–80).

Not suitable for freezing.

Gobi Andey

(Cauliflower with Eggs)

Serves 4

An unusual and delicious way to serve cauliflower, this recipe is from my mother's repertoire. Not only does it taste good, it is also packed with protein and vitamins.

3 tablespoons sunflower or corn oil
1 teaspoon cumin seeds
1 teaspoon coriander seeds, pounded to a medium
coarse texture
½ teaspoon onion seeds (kalonji)
1 onion (about 175g/6oz), finely sliced
1–2 green chillies, seeded and cut into juliennes
¼–½ teaspoon crushed dried red chillies
½ teaspoon ground turmeric
1 medium cauliflower, 500g/1lb when outer leaves
removed, cut into 2.5cm/1 inch florets
½ teaspoon salt or to taste
2 tablespoons chopped coriander leaves
4 eggs (size 2), lightly beaten

1. Preheat a karahi or wok over medium heat for 1–2 minutes, then add the oil. When hot but not smoking, add the cumin and coriander, followed by the onion seeds. Let them sizzle for 10–15 seconds.

2. Add the onion and green chillies. Increase the heat slightly and stir-fry for 4–5 minutes. Add the red chillies and turmeric and stir-fry for 1 minute.

3. Add the cauliflower and stir-fry for 3–4 minutes. Stir in the salt, stir and reduce the heat to low. Cover the karahi or wok with a piece of foil or a lid, and cook for 10–12 minutes. By this time the cauliflower should be tender but still firm, and you will have all the natural juices in the karahi.

4. Stir in the coriander leaves and increase the heat to medium. Pour the beaten eggs evenly over the cauliflower, allow to set for 1 minute, then stir until the eggs coat the cauliflower. Remove from the heat and serve.

Preparation time: 15 minutes

Cooking time: 20 minutes

Serving ideas: Serve with Tarka Dhal (pages 121–2) and Sada Chawal (pages 160–61). A raita is an optional extra.

Variation: Use broccoli instead of cauliflower.

Mattar-Paneer-Makki

(Peas with Indian Cheese and Sweetcorn)

Serves 4–6

Mattar-Paneer is a very popular dish in Northern India, especially in the state of Punjab. I have added sweetcorn (makki) to the traditional combination.

4 tablespoons sunflower or corn oil
250g/8oz paneer, cut into 2.5cm/1 inch cubes
1 teaspoon shahi jeera (royal cumin)
1 onion (about 175g/6oz), finely chopped
5–6 cloves garlic, peeled and crushed
2.5cm/1 inch cube root ginger, peeled and finely grated
1 tablespoon ground coriander
1½ teaspoons ground cumin
1 teaspoon ground turmeric
½ teaspoon chilli powder
1 tablespoon tomato purée
250g/8oz frozen sweetcorn, thawed, or canned
    sweetcorn, drained and rinsed
150g/5oz frozen garden peas, thawed, or cooked fresh
    peas
300ml/½ pint warm water

63

75g/3oz canned chopped tomatoes

1 tablespoon Kasoori methi (dried fenugreek leaves),
   dried stalks removed

½ teaspoon dried mint

1 teaspoon salt or to taste

150ml/¼ pint single cream

3–4 green chillies

2 tablespoons chopped coriander leaves

1. Preheat a karahi or wok over medium heat and add the oil. When hot but not smoking, stir-fry the paneer cubes until golden brown. Take care while frying paneer, as the oil tends to splatter quite a bit. Drain on absorbent paper.

2. Allow the oil to cool slightly, removing the pan from the heat if necessary. Add the shahi jeera and stir-fry for 15 seconds. Add the onion, increase the heat slightly, and stir-fry for 4–5 minutes.

3. Add the garlic, ginger, coriander and cumin, reduce the heat slightly and stir-fry for 1 minute. Add 2 tablespoons water and stir-fry until the water evaporates.

4. Add the turmeric and chilli powder and stir-fry for 30 seconds. Add 2 tablespoons water and stir-fry again until the water evaporates.

5. Add the tomato purée, stir-fry for 30 seconds, then add the sweetcorn, peas and water. Bring to the boil, reduce the heat to low and simmer for 5 minutes.

6. Add the fried paneer, tomatoes, kasoori methi, mint, salt, cream and chillies. Increase the heat slightly and cook for

5 minutes. Stir in the coriander leaves and remove from the heat.

Preparation time: 15–20 minutes
Cooking time: 30 minutes
Serving ideas: Serve with Kesari Chawal (pages 162–3) or Peshawari Naan (pages 173–5), accompanied by a raita.

Saag-Aloo

(Spinach with Potatoes)

Serves 4–6

Spinach leaves collected straight from the garden, glistening with morning dew, is one of my early childhood memories. If you do not have time to prepare fresh spinach which needs thorough cleaning and washing, you can use frozen leaf spinach, but not the purée. You will also need to thaw and drain it well.

375g/13oz old potatoes, peeled and cut into 5cm/2 inch cubes
300ml/½ pint water
3 tablespoons sunflower or corn oil
½ teaspoon black mustard seeds
½ teaspoon fennel seeds
¼–½ teaspoon crushed dried chillies
8 cloves garlic, peeled and crushed
1 onion (about 175g/6oz), finely sliced
½ teaspoon ground fennel
1½ teaspoons ground cumin
½ teaspoon ground turmeric
275g/10oz spinach, finely chopped

1 teaspoon salt or to taste

150g/5oz canned chopped tomatoes, including juice

½ teaspoon Balti Garam Masala (pages 28–9)

1 tablespoon tomato purée

1. Put the potatoes and water in a saucepan over a high heat and bring to the boil. Reduce the heat to medium, cover and cook for 5 minutes or until the potatoes are tender. Remove the potatoes with a slotted spoon and spread on a large plate to prevent cooking further. Reserve the liquid.

2. Preheat a karahi or wok over medium heat for 1–2 minutes, then add the oil. When hot but not smoking, add the mustard seeds and as soon as they pop, add the fennel, crushed chillies and garlic. Stir-fry for 30 seconds.

3. Add the onion and stir-fry for 4–5 minutes or until soft and just beginning to colour.

4. Add the ground fennel, cumin and turmeric, and stir-fry for 1 minute. Add the spinach and salt, and stir-fry for 3 minutes until the spinach has shrunk to half the original amount.

5. Add the tomatoes, potatoes, reserved cooking liquid, garam masala and tomato purée. Increase the heat to high and cook for 4 minutes, stirring frequently, then remove from the heat and serve.

Preparation time: 25 minutes

Cooking time: 25 minutes

Serving ideas: Serve with Peshawari Naan (pages 173–5) and Dhal Makhani (pages 123–4).

Suitable for freezing before adding the potatoes; add them during reheating.

What to do with leftovers: If you have any leftover dhal, mix it with your leftover Saag-Aloo to create a wholesome new dish. Simply heat about 2 teaspoons of oil in a karahi, add ¼ teaspoon Balti Garam Masala (pages 28–9), then add your leftovers and stir-fry until heated through.

Bandhgobi Bhaji

(Dry Spiced Cabbage)

Serves 4–6

A delicious way to cook cabbage – the spicing is subtle and the cabbage is cooked in its own juices. Do try and use red onion as it looks attractive and adds a distinctive flavour. It is expensive, but you only need one.

> 3 tablespoons sunflower or corn oil
> 1 teaspoon cumin seeds
> 1 onion (preferably red), finely sliced
> 6 cloves garlic, peeled and crushed
> 1 green chilli, seeded and cut into juliennes
> ¼ teaspoon ground turmeric
> 500g/1¼lb green cabbage, finely shredded
> 1 teaspoon salt or to taste
> 1 tablespoon chopped coriander leaves

1. Preheat a karahi or wok over medium heat for 1–2 minutes then add the oil. When hot but not smoking, add the cumin seeds and allow to sizzle for 15 seconds.
2. Add the onion, garlic and chilli. Stir-fry for 4 minutes and add turmeric. Stir fry for 30 seconds.

69

3. Add the cabbage and salt, stir-fry for 2 minutes then reduce the heat to low. Cover the karahi or wok with a piece of foil or lid, and cook the cabbage in its own juices for 10–12 minutes. If you like the cabbage really soft, cook for 15 minutes. Stir in the coriander leaves, remove from the heat and serve.

Preparation time: 20 minutes

Cooking time: 20–25 minutes

Serving ideas: Serve with Kashmir ki Roti (page s 168–9) accompanied by any dhal and a raita.

Suitable for freezing.

Variation: Use 2.5cm/1 inch cauliflower florets instead of cabbage.

Palak Paneer

(Spinach with Indian Cheese)

Serves 4

This is one of those all-in-one dishes which provides you with protein, carbohydrate, vitamins and minerals. Paneer is easy to make at home (see pages 30–31) but if you do not have the time, you can buy it from good supermarkets and Asian shops.

    4 tablespoons sunflower or corn oil
    250g/8oz paneer, cut into 1cm/½ inch cubes
    6 cloves garlic, peeled and crushed
    1 small onion (about 100g/4oz), very finely chopped
    2.5cm/1 inch cube root ginger, peeled and finely grated
    1 tablespoon ground coriander
    1 teaspoon ground cumin
    10g/4oz canned chopped tomatoes including juice
    ½ teaspoon ground turmeric
    1 teaspoon paprika
    ¼–½ teaspoon chilli powder
    150g/5oz spinach, finely chopped, or frozen leaf spinach,
        thawed and drained
    300ml/½ pint warm water
    175g/6oz boiled potatoes, cut into 2.5cm/1 inch cubes

71

1 teaspoon salt or to taste

½ teaspoon Balti Garam Masala (pages 28–9)

4 tablespoons single cream

1. Preheat a karahi or wok over medium heat for 1–2 minutes. Add 2 tablespoons of the oil. When hot but not smoking, fry the cubes of paneer until lightly browned, tossing and turning them constantly. This will only take 1½–2 minutes. Drain on absorbent paper.

2. Add the remaining oil to the karahi or wok and heat for a minute or so. Add the garlic and stir-fry for 30 seconds, then add the onion and stir-fry for 2 minutes.

3. Add the ginger, ground coriander and cumin, stir-fry for 30 seconds and add the tomatoes. Stir-fry for 2 minutes or until the oil floats on top.

4. Add the turmeric, paprika and chilli powder and stir-fry for 30 seconds. Add the spinach and stir-fry for 2–3 minutes, then add half the water. Cook for 3 minutes or until the water dries up, tossing and turning the ingredients constantly.

5. Add the fried paneer, potatoes, salt and remaining water. Cook for 1 minute, then reduce the heat to low and simmer for 5 minutes, uncovered. Add a little more water if necessary.

6. Sprinkle on the garam masala, stir in the cream, remove from the heat and serve.

Preparation time: 25–30 minutes

Cooking time: 20 minutes

Serving ideas: Serve with Peshawari Naan (pages 173–5) and a
  raita.

Suitable for freezing (the texture of the cooked potatoes will
  change when thawed).

Variations: Use frozen garden peas instead of spinach, thaw
  them first. Fresh peas are lovely and should be cooked
  before adding to the sauce.

  Use tofu instead of paneer.

Bhindi Mirchiwali

⬚ V ⬚

(Okra with Peppers)

Serves 4

A light and aromatic dish with an attractive appearance. The soft green colour of the okra contrasts beautifully with the bright red sweet pepper and sliced onions, and the entire combination in a little creamy sauce looks stunning.

> 225g/8oz bhindi (okra)
> 1 red pepper (about 150g/5oz)
> 1 onion (about 175g/6oz)
> 1 tablespoon white poppy seeds
> 1 tablespoon sesame seeds
> 1 long slim dried red chilli, chopped
> 3 tablespoons sunflower or corn oil
> 4–5 cloves garlic, peeled and crushed
> ½ teaspoon salt or to taste
> 75ml/3 fl oz warm water

1. Scrub each okra gently, rinse well in running water, then slice off the hard head.
2. Halve the pepper and remove the seeds and white pith. Cut into 4cm/1½ inch strips.

3. Peel and halve the onion lengthwise, then cut into 5mm/¼ inch thick slices.

4. Grind the poppy seeds, sesame seeds and red chilli in a coffee grinder until fine.

5. Preheat a karahi or wok over medium heat and add the oil. When hot but not smoking, stir-fry the garlic for 30 seconds or until beginning to brown.

6. Add the onion and stir-fry for 2–3 minutes, then add the ground ingredients. Stir-fry for 30 seconds.

7. Add the okra and salt, stir-fry for 30 seconds and add the water. Reduce the heat to low, cover the pan with a piece of foil or a lid, and cook for 5 minutes.

8. Stir in the red pepper, cover again and cook for 4–5 minutes. Remove from the heat and serve.

Preparation time: 20–25 minutes

Cooking time: 15 minutes

Serving ideas: Serve with Sada Chawal (pages 160–61) accompanied by Dhal Makhani (pages 123–4) and Ghia ka Raita (pages 186–7).

Suitable for freezing.

Variation: Use whole green beans instead of okra.

Bandhgobi aur Moong Dhal Jhal Frazi

(Stir-fried Cabbage with Lentils)

Serves 4–6

Moong dhal is one of the fastest cooking lentils and it has a delicious earthy flavour. All Asian stores and some health food shops stock moong dhal. It is also known as yellow split lentils. Jhal frazi is akin to stir-frying which suits Balti recipes perfectly.

4 tablespoons sunflower or corn oil
1 large onion (about 225g/8oz), finely chopped
1 teaspoon shahi jeera (royal cumin)
6 cloves garlic, peeled and crushed
1cm/½ inch cube root ginger, peeled and grated
1 green chilli, seeded and chopped
¼ teaspoon crushed dried chillies (optional)
100g/4oz moong dhal, picked over, washed and soaked
   for 1 hour, drained
½ teaspoon ground turmeric
300ml/½ pint warm water
350g/12oz green cabbage, finely shredded
1 teaspoon salt or to taste
1½ teaspoon ground cumin
2 tablespoons chopped coriander leaves

1. Preheat the karahi or wok over a medium heat for 1–2 minutes, then add the oil. When hot, stir-fry the onion for 8–10 minutes golden brown. Tilt the pan and squeeze out as much oil as possible from the onion by pressing onto the side with a spoon. Drain on absorbent paper.

2. Reduce the heat slightly, and fry the shahi jeera in the remaining oil for 15 seconds.

3. Add the garlic, ginger, fresh chilli and crushed chillies (if used). Stir-fry for 30 seconds and add the drained dhal. Stir-fry for 1½ minutes, reduce heat to low and stir-fry for a further 1½ minutes.

4. Add the ground turmeric, stir-fry for 30 seconds, then add the water and half the fried onions. Increase the heat to medium and cook for 5 minutes, stirring frequently.

5. Add the cabbage and salt and stir-fry for 5 minutes.

6. Add the cumin, stir-fry for 2 minutes then add the coriander. Stir-fry for 1 minute and remove from the heat. Serve garnished with the remaining fried onions.

Preparation time: 15–20 minutes, plus soaking dhal
Cooking time: 25 minutes
Serving ideas: Serve with Balti Naan (pages 170–72) and Do-Piaza Khumb (pages 92–4).
Suitable for freezing.

Shalgam ka Salan

(Spiced Turnips)

Serves 4–6

In this superbly flavoured dish, turnips are first fried in ghee then simmered gently in a spice-laced yogurt sauce which complements the natural flavour of the vegetable beautifully.

700g/1½lb turnips
175g/6oz thick set whole milk natural yogurt
50g/2oz ghee
1 onion (about 175g/6oz), finely sliced
1 teaspoon shahi jeera (royal cumin)
4 whole cloves
1cm/½ inch cube root ginger, peeled and cut into
    juliennes
2 teaspoons ground coriander
½ teaspoon ground turmeric
¼–½ teaspoon chilli powder
1 teaspoon salt or to taste
300ml/½ pint warm water
½ teaspoon Balti Garam Masala (pages 28–9)
1–2 green chillies, seeded and cut into juliennes
2 tablespoons chopped coriander leaves

1. Trim, peel and wash the turnips and wash. Cut each one into half, then quarter each half so that you have approximately 4cm/1½ inch chunks.
2. Put the yogurt in a bowl and beat until smooth. Set aside.
3. Preheat a karahi or wok over medium-high heat for 1–2 minutes, then add the ghee. When hot, stir-fry the turnips in batches until they are well browned. Each batch will take 6–7 minutes. Drain on absorbent paper.
4. Reduce the heat slightly, add the onion to the pan and fry until lightly browned, about 8–9 minutes. Remove the pan from the heat and tilt to one side, squeezing out as much ghee as possible from the onion by pressing it to the side of the pan with a spoon. Drain the onion on absorbent paper.
5. Return the pan to low heat. In the ghee left in the pan, fry the shahi jeera for 15 seconds, then add the cloves and ginger. Stir fry for 30 seconds.
6. Add the coriander, turmeric and chilli powder and stir-fry for 30 seconds. Make sure the pan is not too hot, if it is, remove from the heat and cool for a minute or so. Add half the yogurt and bring to a very slow simmer. Now add the remaining yogurt and let it bubble very gently until the ghee rises to the top.
7. Add the fried turnips, fried onions, salt and water. Stir and mix well. Cover with a piece of foil or a lid, and simmer very gently for 25–30 minutes or until the turnips are tender.
8. Add the garam masala, chillies and coriander leaves. Stir, remove from heat and serve.

79

Preparation time: 15 minutes

Cooking time: 50–55 minutes

Serving ideas: Serve with Dhal Makhani (pages 123–4) and
   Balti Naan (pages 170–72).

Variation: Substitute half the turnips with potatoes.

Use suran (yam) instead of turnips.

Suitable for freezing.

Dum-Aloo Dalchini

(New Potatoes with Cinnamon)

Serves 4

Packed with wonderful aromatic spices, this is a lovely way to serve new potatoes. I have used ghee for a richer flavour, but you can use oil if you wish. Butter is not suitable because of the fairly high temperature needed to fry the potatoes. You can, however, use a mixture of oil and butter.

4500g/1lb small new potatoes
50g/2oz ghee
1 teaspoon fennel seeds
4 x 2.5cm/1 inch pieces cassia bark or cinnamon sticks
6 whole cloves
2 bay leaves, crumbled
1 large onion (about 225g/8oz), finely chopped
4cm/1½ inch cube root ginger, peeled and finely grated
½ teaspoon ground fennel
½ teaspoon ground turmeric
2 teaspoons ground cumin
¼–½ teaspoon chilli powder
100g/4oz canned chopped tomatoes including juice
1 teaspoon salt or to taste

81

600ml/1 pint warm water

½ teaspoon dried mint or 1 tablespoon finely chopped
  fresh mint

75ml/3 fl oz single cream

½ teaspoon Balti Garam Masala (pages 28–9)

2 tablespoons chopped coriander leaves

1. Scrub or scrape the potatoes, wash and dry thoroughly. Using a sharp knife, make several deep incisions in each potato without cutting right through. This will enable the flavours to penetrate the potatoes.

2. Preheat a karahi or wok over medium-high heat for 1–2 minutes, then add the ghee. When hot, fry the potatoes, in batches if necessary, until well browned. Each batch will take 8–10 minutes. Keep moving them around the pan to ensure even browning, they will brown very quickly towards the end. Turn off the heat and remove the potatoes with a slotted spoon and drain on absorbent paper. Let the fat cool for a minute or so then turn on the heat to low.

3. Add the fennel, cassia or cinnamon, cloves and bay leaves, and stir-fry for 15 seconds. Do not worry if you have browned potato crust in the pan, this will add plenty of flavour to the dish.

4. Increase the heat to medium and add the onion and ginger. Stir-fry for 4–5 minutes or until the onion is soft.

5. Add the ground fennel, turmeric, cumin and chilli powder. Stir-fry for 30 seconds and add the tomatoes. Stir-fry for 2–3 minutes or until the fat rises to the top.

6. Add the fried potatoes, salt and water. Bring to the boil and cook for 2 minutes. Stir once to re-position the potatoes, then reduce the heat to low. Cover the pan with a piece of foil or a lid and simmer for 20 minutes. Stir occasionally and re-position potatoes.

7. Add the mint and cream and increase the heat to medium. Cook for 5 minutes. Stir in the garam masala and coriander leaves, remove from the heat and serve.

Preparation time: 25 minutes

Cooking time: 50–55 minutes

Serving ideas: Serve with Peshawari Naan (pages 173–5) and Tarka Dhal (pages 121–2) or Dhal Panchrattan (pages 117–18).

Not suitable for freezing.

Aloo Ki Bhaji

$\boxed{\text{V}}$

(Spiced Potatoes)

Serves 4

The word 'bhaji' is often confused with 'bhajiya' in this country. This is due to the way 'onion bhaji', a deep fried snack, is spelt on some restaurant menus. Bhaji is a traditional vegetable dish with little or no sauce.

> 4 tablespoons sunflower or corn oil
> ½ teaspoon black mustard seeds
> 1 teaspoon cumin seeds
> 8–10 curry leaves (optional)
> 1 onion (about 175g/6oz), finely sliced
> 1–2 green chillies, seeded and finely chopped
> 1 tablespoon dhanna-jeera powder
> 1 teaspoon ground turmeric
> ¼–½ teaspoon chilli powder (optional)
> 2 small ripe tomatoes, skinned and chopped
> 1 teaspoon salt or to taste
> 450g/1lb old potatoes, boiled, peeled and cut into 2.5cm/
>   1 inch cubes
> 300ml/½ pint warm water
> 2 tablespoons finely chopped coriander leaves

1. Preheat a karahi or wok over medium heat for 1–2 minutes, then add the oil. When hot but not smoking, add the mustard seeds. As soon as they pop, add the cumin and curry leaves (if used). Immediately follow with the onion and chillies, and stir-fry for 5–6 minutes or until the onion begins to colour.
2. Add the dhanna-jeera powder, turmeric and chilli powder (if used). Stir-fry for 30 seconds, add the tomatoes and stir-fry for 1 minute.
3. Add the salt, potatoes and water, stir and cook for 4–5 minutes.
4. Stir in the coriander leaves, remove from the heat and serve.

Preparation time: 20–25 minutes, plus time to boil potatoes
Cooking time: 10–12 minutes
Serving ideas: Serve with Balti Naan (pages 170–72) or
    Methi ki Roti (pages 176–7).
Not suitable for freezing.

Kaddu Malai

(Creamed Butternut Squash)

Serves 4–6

One of my lovely childhood memories came flooding back when I was testing this recipe. My mother cooked this dish to perfection, using pumpkin, in a blackened heavy cast iron karahi. The rich golden colour of the pumpkin showed off beautifully in the black karahi and it made a pretty picture with fresh coriander leaves on top.

> 1 butternut squash or a small pumpkin (about 550g/1¼lb)
> 2 potatoes (about 200g/7oz)
> 50g/2oz ghee or unsalted butter
> 2 x 2.5cm/1 inch pieces cassia bark or cinnamon sticks
> 4 green cardamom pods, split to the top of each pod
> 4 whole cloves
> 8 cloves garlic, peeled and crushed
> 1 small onion (about 100g/4oz), finely chopped
> 1 tablespoon ground cumin
> 1 teaspoon ground turmeric
> ½–1 teaspoon crushed dried red chillies
> 100g/4oz canned chopped tomatoes including juice

2.5cm/1 inch cube root ginger, peeled and grated

1 teaspoon salt or to taste

350ml/12 fl oz warm water

½ teaspoon Balti Garam Masala (pages 28–9)

75ml/3 fl oz single cream

2 tablespoon finely chopped coriander leaves

1. Halve or quarter the butternut squash or pumpkin and remove the seeds. Peel and cut into 2.5cm/1 inch cubes.

2. Peel the potatoes and cut into 1cm/½ inch cubes.

3. Preheat a karahi or wok over medium heat for 1–2 minutes, then add the ghee or butter. When melted, add the cassia or cinnamon, cardamom and cloves. Let the spices sizzle for 30 seconds.

4. Add the garlic, stir-fry for 30 seconds, then add the onion. Stir-fry for 4–5 minutes or until the onion begins to colour.

5. Add the cumin, turmeric and crushed chillies, stir-fry for 30 seconds and add the tomatoes. Stir-fry for 4–5 minutes or until the oil separates from the spice paste and begins to float.

6. Add the ginger, stir-fry for 1 minute then add the pumpkin, potatoes, salt and water. Increase the heat to high, bring to the boil and cook for 2–3 minutes. Now reduce the heat to low and cover the pan with a lid or a piece of foil. Cook for 20–25 minutes, stirring occasionally.

7. Add the garam masala, cream and half the coriander leaves. Stir and cook for 1 minute, then remove from

the heat. Serve garnished with the remaining coriander leaves.

Preparation time: 20–25 minutes

Cooking time: 40 minutes

Serving ideas: Serve with Balti Naan (pages 170–72) or Kashmiri Roti (pages 168–9) and Moong Dhal Jhal Frazi (pages 76–7).

Suitable for freezing, though the texture of cooked potatoes will change slightly.

Brinjal Bhaji

(Spiced Aubergine)

Serves 4–6

I tasted this lovely dish at the Balti restaurant in King's Road, London, called 'Planet Pappodum'. The chef there was very secretive about his recipe, but was kind enough to show me the dish at different cooking stages. When I came home, I worked on it straightaway and here is my version.

2 large aubergines (about 550g/1¼lb total)
1 large onion (about 250g/8oz), roughly chopped
2.5cm/1 inch cube root ginger, peeled and roughly chopped
6 cloves garlic, peeled and roughly chopped
1–2 long slim dried red chillies, roughly chopped
3–4 tablespoons water
4 tablespoons sunflower or corn oil
½ teaspoon black mustard seeds
½ teaspoon cumin seeds
½ teaspoon ground fennel
1 teaspoon ground coriander
½ teaspoon ground cumin
1 teaspoon ground turmeric

150g/5oz canned chopped tomatoes including juice
1 teaspoon salt or to taste
1 tablespoon tomato purée
450ml/¾ pint warm water
½ teaspoon Balti Garam Masala (pages 28–9)
2 tablespoons finely chopped coriander leaves

1. Quarter the aubergines lengthwise, then cut each quarter lengthwise into half. Cut into 2.5cm/1 inch chunks and soak in salted water for 30 minutes. Drain and rinse well.

2. Purée the onions, ginger, garlic and red chillies with the 3–4 tablespoons water in a food processor or liquidizer.

3. Preheat a karahi or wok over medium heat for 1–2 minutes, then add the oil. When hot but not smoking, add the mustard seeds. As soon as they pop, add the cumin seeds and stir-fry for 15 seconds.

4. Add the puréed ingredients and stir-fry for 2 minutes. Reduce the heat to low and stir-fry for a further 2 minutes.

5. Add the ground fennel, coriander, cumin and turmeric. Stir-fry for 2 minutes and add half the tomatoes. Increase the heat to medium and stir-fry for 2–3 minutes. Add the remaining tomatoes and stir-fry for a further 2–3 minutes or until the oil separates from the spice paste.

6. Add the salt, tomato purée, warm water and aubergine, stir once, and bring to the boil. Reduce the heat to medium and cook for 10 minutes, uncovered. Stir well several times to ensure even cooking. The aubergine will float on the liquid during this time. When it begins to soak

up the liquid, it will sink. When this happens, reduce the heat to low and simmer for 5 minutes, stirring well 2–3 times.

7. Sprinkle with the garam masala and coriander leaves. Stir again, remove from the heat and serve.

Preparation time: 15 minutes, plus soaking aubergine
Cooking time: 30 minutes
Serving ideas: Serve with Balti Naan (pages 170–72) accompanied by a protein-rich dish such as Dhal Makhani (pages 123–4) or Dhal Panchrattan (pages 117–18).
Not suitable for freezing.

Do-Piaza Khumb $\boxed{\text{V}}$

(Mushroom Do-Piaza)

Serves 4

Mushrooms grow abundantly in Baltistan and its neighbouring areas. Do-Piaza is a Mogul term and it means any meat cooked with vegetables with lashings of onions. However, I have created this vegetarian version with mushrooms as the main ingredient.

1 small onion (about 100g/4oz), roughly chopped
1cm/½ inch cube root ginger, peeled and roughly
   chopped
4 cloves garlic, peeled and chopped
1 green chilli, seeded and chopped
3–4 tablespoons water
4 tablespoons sunflower or corn oil
1 small onion (about 100g/4oz), very finely chopped
2 teaspoons ground coriander
1½ teaspoons ground cumin
¼ teaspoon crushed dried chillies
1 teaspoon ground turmeric
10g/4oz canned chopped tomatoes including juice
1 tablespoon tomato purée

1 teaspoon salt or to taste

375g/13oz closed cup mushrooms, thickly sliced

90g/3½oz frozen garden peas or cooked fresh peas

75ml/3 fl oz warm water

½ teaspoon Balti Garam Masala (pages 28–9)

1. Purée the onion, ginger, garlic and fresh chilli with the 3–4 tablespoons of water in a food processor or liquidizer.
2. Preheat a karahi or wok over medium heat and add the oil. When hot but not smoking, add the chopped onion and stir-fry for 3–4 minutes or until beginning to colour.
3. Add the ground coriander, cumin and crushed chillies. Stir-fry for 30 seconds, then add the puréed ingredients and stir-fry over a low heat for 3–4 minutes.
4. Add the turmeric and half the tomatoes, increase the heat to medium, and stir-fry for 2–3 minutes. Add the remaining tomatoes and stir-fry for 2–3 minutes or until the oil separates from the spice paste.
5. Add the tomato purée, salt, mushrooms, peas and warm water, stir and mix well. Reduce the heat to low and simmer, uncovered, for 5–6 minutes. By this time, the natural juices from the mushrooms, combined with the little cooking liquid will produce a thick, paste-like sauce.
6. Sprinkle with the garam masala and stir-fry for 1 minute. Remove from the heat and serve.

Preparation time: 20–25 minutes

Cooking time: 20 minutes

Serving ideas: Serve with Balti Naan (pages 170–72) or
  Peshawari Naan (pages 173–5) and Channa Dhal Masala
  (pages 114–16).
Suitable for freezing.
Variation: Use cooked sliced green beans instead of peas.

Peshawari Paneer

(Peshawar-style Spiced Cheese)

Serves 4

Peshawar, in northern Pakistan, is said to be one of the original homes of Balti/karahi cooking. I have named this recipe such as a tribute to Peshawar.

50g/2oz ghee or unsalted butter

200g/7oz paneer, cut into 2.5cm/1 inch cubes

2 x 2.5cm/1 inch pieces cassia bark or cinnamon sticks

4 cardamom pods, split to the top of each pod

8 cloves garlic, peeled and pounded to a pulp

1 onion (about 175g/6oz), finely chopped

1 green chilli, seeded and cut into juliennes

1 tablespoon dhanna-jeera powder

½ teaspoon ground turmeric

¼–½ teaspoon chilli powder

150g/5oz canned chopped tomatoes including juice

1 tablespoon mint leaves, finely chopped or ½ teaspoon
dried mint

75g/3oz frozen garden peas, thawed, or cooked fresh peas

185g/6oz frozen sweetcorn, thawed, or canned sweetcorn, drained and rinsed

40g/1½oz raw cashews, split
25g/1oz seedless raisins
1 teaspoon salt or to taste
350ml/12 fl oz warm water
½ teaspoon Balti Garam Masala (pages 28–9)

1. Preheat a karahi or wok over medium heat for 1–2 minutes, then add the ghee or butter. When hot, turn the heat down to low and fry the cubes of paneer, in batches if necessary, until lightly browned. Drain on absorbent paper.

2. In the same fat, fry the cassia and cardamom for 15 seconds. Add the garlic and stir-fry for 30 seconds or until lightly browned.

3. Add the onions and chilli and increase the heat to medium. Stir-fry for 4 minutes or until the onions are soft and just beginning to colour.

4. Add the dhanna-jeera powder, turmeric and chilli powder. Stir-fry for 1 minute and add tomatoes and mint. Stir fry for 1 minute.

5. Add the peas, sweetcorn, cashews, raisins and salt. Stir-fry for 2 minutes, then add the water and cook for 2 minutes.

6. Add the paneer, cover the pan with a lid or a piece of foil and reduce the heat to low. Cook for 5 minutes.

7. Sprinkle with the garam masala, stir, remove from heat and serve.

Preparation time: 20–25 minutes

Cooking time: 18–20 minutes

Serving ideas: Serve with Balti Naan (pages 170–72) or Soda Naan (pages 178–80).

Variation: Use tofu instead of paneer.

Khumb-Aloo $\boxed{V}$

(Mushrooms with Potatoes)

Serves 4–6

Another delicious dish which I first tasted at the Planet Poppodum restaurant in London. The chef used closed cup mushrooms, but I prefer the texture and flavour of the large open cap mushrooms when they are combined with potatoes. You can, of course, use either.

350g/12oz large open cap mushrooms
1 onion (about 175g/6oz), roughly chopped
5–6 cloves garlic, peeled and roughly chopped
2.5cm/1 inch cube root ginger, peeled and roughly
    chopped
3 tablespoons sunflower or corn oil
2 tablespoons tomato purée
200g/7oz canned chopped tomatoes including juice
1½ teaspoons ground cumin
2 teaspoons ground coriander
½–1 teaspoon chilli powder
1 teaspoon ground turmeric
1 teaspoon salt or to taste
275ml/8 fl oz warm water

225g/8oz old potatoes, boiled, peeled and cut into
    2.5cm/1 inch cubes
½ teaspoon dried mint
¼ teaspoon Balti Garam Masala (pages 28–9)
2 tablespoons finely chopped coriander leaves

1. Quarter the mushrooms and cut each quarter into two.
2. Purée the onion, garlic and ginger with the 3–4 tablespoons of water in a blender or food processor.
3. Preheat a karahi or wok over medium heat for 1–2 minutes, then add the oil. When hot but not smoking, add the puréed ingredients and stir-fry for 3–4 minutes.
4. Add the tomato purée and stir-fry for 1 minute, then add half the tomatoes. Stir-fry for 1 minute.
5. Add the ground cumin, coriander, chilli powder and turmeric. Stir-fry for 1 minute, then add the remaining tomatoes. Stir-fry for a further minute, making sure you scrape and mix any spice paste that sticks to the bottom of the pan. This will add extra flavour to the dish.
6. Add the mushrooms, salt and water, cook for 2 minutes, and reduce the heat to low. Cover the karahi or wok with a lid or a piece of foil and simmer for 5 minutes.
7. Add the potatoes and mint, cover again and simmer for 3–4 minutes.
8. Sprinkle with the garam masala and fresh coriander. Stir, remove from the heat and serve.

Preparation time: 15–20 minutes, plus boiling potatoes
Cooking time: 18–20 minutes

Serving ideas: Serve with Balti Naan (pages 170–72) and
Rajma Masala (pages 119–20) or other protein-rich dish.

Suitable for freezing before adding the potatoes.

What to do with leftovers: Besides reheating to use as before, you
can mix it with Sada Chawal (pages 160–61) to make a
delicious instant mushroom pulao. Garnish with fresh
coriander and serve with Dhal Makhani (pages 123–4) and
a raita. There is no hard and fast rule about the proportion
of cooked vegetables to rice. You can use as much or as
little as you like to freshly cooked Basmati rice.

Sabzi Besan Ki

$\boxed{\text{V}}$

(Vegetables with Gram Flour)

Serves 4–6

'Besan', a special flour made of dried gram or chick peas, is available in Asian stores, health food shops and some good supermarkets. It can be stored like ordinary flour, in a cool dry place.

4 leeks (about 450g/1lb)
1 red pepper (about 200g/7oz)
4 tablespoons sunflower or corn oil
½ teaspoon black mustard seeds
½ teaspoon cumin seeds
10–12 fenugreek seeds
8 cloves garlic, peeled and crushed
¼ teaspoon crushed dried red chillies
1 teaspoon salt or to taste
2 tablespoon chopped coriander leaves
125g/4oz besan (gram flour), sifted

1. Trim the leeks and halve them lengthwise. Wash thoroughly making sure you remove any grit between the leaves. Holding 3–4 halves of leeks together, slice them finely.

101

2. Remove the seeds and pith from the pepper and cut into 2.5cm/1 inch strips.

3. Preheat a karahi or wok over medium heat for 1–2 minutes, then add the oil. When hot but not smoking, reduce the heat slightly and add the mustard seeds. As soon as they pop, add the cumin and fenugreek and follow with the garlic. Stir-fry for 1 minute.

4. Add the crushed chillies, stir-fry for 30 seconds and add the leeks, pepper slices and salt. Increase the heat to medium and stir-fry for 5 minutes.

5. Add the coriander leaves and 2 tablespoons of water, then sprinkle the besan evenly over the vegetables. Stir-fry for 1½ minutes and remove from the heat. Scrape off and mix any besan that sticks to the bottom of the pan. This will add extra flavour.

Preparation time: 20 minutes

Cooking time: 10 minutes

Serving ideas: Serve with Kashmir ki Roti (pages 168–9) or Sada Chawal (pages 160–61) and Aloo Choley (pages 146–8).

Not suitable for freezing.

What to do with leftovers: Use as a filling for spicy toasted sandwiches (excellent made in an electric toasted sandwich maker).

Variation: Add equal quantities of onion and cabbage instead of leeks. Stir-fry the onions for 2–3 minutes before adding the cabbage and pepper slices.

Shakahari Rogan Josh

(Vegetarian Rogan Josh)

Serves 4–6

Rogan Josh, a famous Kashmiri dish, is equally popular in India and abroad. I have created this vegetarian version using soya chunks. Soya is nutritious, tasty and very versatile. You can buy soya chunks from health food shops. They are made of dehydrated soya bean flour and you need to re-hydrate them before cooking. The process is very simple.

100g/4oz soya chunks
2 tablespoons sunflower or soya oil
75g/3oz ghee or unsalted butter
5–6 cloves garlic, peeled and crushed to a pulp
4cm/1½ inch cube root ginger, peeled and finely grated
1 large onion (about 225g/8oz), finely chopped
2 teaspoons ground cumin
2 teaspoons ground coriander
½ teaspoon ground turmeric
½ teaspoon chilli powder
150g/5oz canned chopped tomatoes including juice
1 tablespoon tomato purée
450ml/¾ pint warm water

103

1 teaspoon salt or to taste
½ teaspoon dried mint
100ml/3½ fl oz/two thirds of one cup single cream
½ teaspoon Balti Garam Masala (pages 28–9)
2 tablespoons chopped coriander leaves

1. Put the soya chunks into a medium-sized bowl and pour in plenty of boiling water. Leave to soak for 30 minutes, then drain thoroughly.
2. Preheat a karahi or wok over medium heat. Add the oil and 25g/1oz ghee or butter. When hot, stir-fry the soya for 4–5 minutes, reduce the heat to low and add the garlic and ginger. Stir fry for 1 minute and remove from the heat. Set aside.
3. Preheat a separate karahi or wok over medium heat and add the remaining ghee or butter. When hot, stir-fry the onion for 4–5 minutes, reduce the heat to low and add the cumin, coriander, turmeric and chilli powder. Stir-fry for 1 minute, then add the tomatoes and tomato purée. Stir-fry for 2 minutes or until the oil surfaces the spice paste. Remove from the heat.
4. Return the pan with the soya chunks to the heat, and add the spice mixture from the other pan. Stir-fry over medium heat for 1 minute, then add the water, salt and mint. Bring to the boil, cover with a piece of foil or a lid, and simmer for 15 minutes.
5. Add the cream and garam masala and simmer for 5 minutes, uncovered. Stir in the coriander leaves, remove from heat and serve.

Preparation time: 15 minutes, plus soaking time for soya
Cooking time: 30 minutes
Serving ideas: Serve with Kesari Chawal (pages 162–3) and
   a raita.

Makki-Khumb Jhal Frazi $\boxed{\text{V}}$

(Sweetcorn and Mushroom Jhal Frazi)

Serves 4–6

A quick and easy dish to prepare with an attractive and colourful appearance. Jhal frazi (a kind of stir-frying) is a style of cooking which suits Balti recipes perfectly.

3 tablespoons cooking oil
1 large onion (about 225g/8oz), finely sliced
2.5cm/1 inch cube root ginger, peeled and finely grated
1 green chilli, seeded and sliced
6 cloves garlic, peeled and crushed
½ teaspoon chilli powder
2 teaspoons ground coriander
1 teaspoon ground cumin
275g/10oz canned chopped tomatoes
225g/8oz frozen sweetcorn, thawed, or canned
    sweetcorn, drained and rinsed
275g/10oz closed cup mushrooms, sliced
1 tablespoon tomato purée
½ teaspoon dried mint
1 tablespoon Kasoori methi, dried stalks removed
50ml/2 fl oz warm water

1 teaspoon salt or to taste

25g/1oz red pepper, diced

25g/1oz green pepper, diced

½ teaspoon Balti Garam Masala (pages 28–9)

1 tablespoon chopped coriander leaves

1. Preheat a karahi or wok over medium heat for 1–2 minutes, then add the oil. When hot, stir-fry the onions for 3–4 minutes or until just beginning to colour.

2. Add the ginger, fresh chilli and garlic, stir-fry for 1 minute and add the chilli powder, coriander and cumin. Stir-fry for 30 seconds.

3. Add half the tomatoes and stir-fry for 2–3 minutes or until the oil surfaces the spice paste.

4. Add the sweetcorn, mushrooms, tomato purée, mint, kasoori methi and water. Stir-fry for 3–4 minutes, then add the salt and red and green pepper, and stir-fry for 1–2 minutes.

5. Add the remaining tomatoes, garam masala and coriander leaves. Stir-fry for 1 minute, remove from the heat and serve.

Preparation time: 15 minutes

Cooking time: 20 minutes

Serving ideas: Serve with Balti Naan (pages 170–72) accompanied by a protein-dish such as Channa Dhal Masala (pages 114–6).

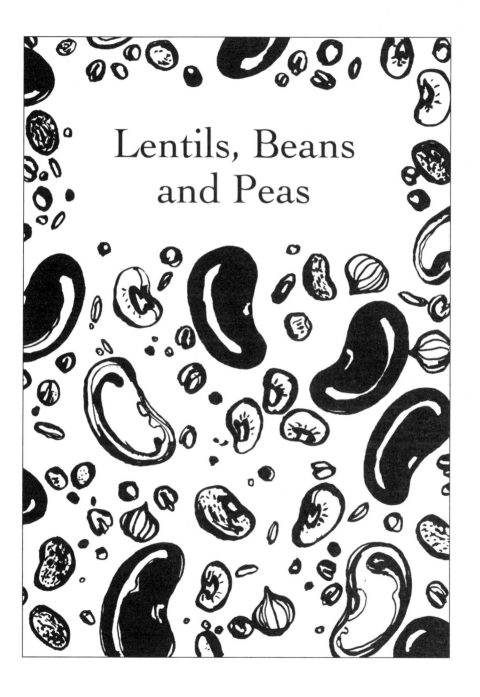

Lentils, Beans
and Peas

Lentils, beans and peas form a very important part of a vegetarian diet. Indian vegetarian food is a classic example of balanced, healthy and appetizing meals. It consists of high protein and high fibre with all the essential vitamins and nutrients.

The main source of protein is grains and pulses. These also have a high content of fibre, vitamins and minerals.

As you will see from the recipes in this chapter, lentils, beans and peas can be cooked in numerous ways to produce delicious and varied meals.

Sabut Mung Sabzi Ke Sath

(Mung Beans with Vegetables)

Serves 4

I have used the Balti combination theme to make this delicious and colourful dish. The onion used in the stir-frying process can be replaced by chopped baby leeks which are wonderful.

150g/5oz mung beans
300ml/½ pint water
2 tablespoons sunflower or corn oil
½ teaspoon black mustard seeds
½ teaspoon cumin seeds
3–4 cloves garlic, peeled and crushed
2.5cm/1 inch cube root ginger, peeled and grated
50g/2oz red pepper, cut into 2.5cm/1 inch dice
1 small onion (about 100g/4oz), coarsely chopped
100g/4oz carrots, halved lengthwise and thinly sliced
100g/4oz cauliflower, divided into 5mm/¼ inch florets
1 teaspoon salt or to taste
½ teaspoon chilli powder
100g/4oz canned chopped tomatoes including juice
2 tablespoons chopped coriander leaves

1. Pick over the mung beans, wash and soak in plenty of cold water overnight. Drain and rinse several times.

2. Put the beans and water in a karahi, wok or saucepan and place over a high heat. Bring to the boil, partially cover the pan and cook over medium heat for 5–6 minutes or until it stops being frothy. Reduce the heat to low, cover and simmer for 15 minutes or until the beans are tender and the liquid reduces to about 2–3 tablespoons.

3. Preheat a karahi or wok over medium heat and add the oil. When hot but not smoking, add the mustard seeds followed by the cumin. As soon as the seeds pop, add the garlic, ginger, red pepper and onion. Stir-fry for 1 minute.

4. Add the carrots and cauliflower, stir-fry for a further minute, then add the salt and chilli powder. Stir-fry for 1–2 minutes.

5. Add the cooked beans, along with the cooking liquid left in the pan. Stir-fry for 2–3 minutes or until the beans and vegetables are well blended.

6. Add the tomatoes and stir-fry for 1–2 minutes. Stir in coriander leaves, remove from the heat and serve.

Preparation time: 25 minutes, plus time for soaking beans
Cooking time: 25 minutes
Serving ideas: Serve with Methi ki Roti (pages 176–7) accompanied by Do-piaza Khumb (pages 92–4).
Suitable for freezing.

Channa Dhal Masala

V

(Spiced Bengal Gram Dhal)

Serves 4

A superb lentil delicacy with the distinctive flavours of fennel and fenugreek (Kasoori methi). If you cannot get channa dhal, use yellow split peas instead, though the latter does not have the same flavour.

175g/6oz channa dhal or yellow split peas

600ml/1 pint water

3 tablespoons sunflower or corn oil

2 x 2.5cm/1 inch pieces cassia bark or cinnamon sticks

1 teaspoon fennel seeds

6–8 cloves garlic, peeled and crushed

½ teaspoon crushed dried chillies

1 onion (about 175g/6oz), finely sliced

1–2 green chillies, seeded and cut into juliennes

1 teaspoon salt or to taste

1 teaspoon ground fennel

1 teaspoon ground cumin

225g/8oz canned chopped tomatoes including juice

1 tablespoon Kasoori methi, dried stalks removed

1 teaspoon Balti Garam Masala (pages 28–9)

2 tablespoons chopped coriander leaves

1. Pick over the dhal and wash in several changes of water. Soak in plenty of cold water for 2 hours. Longer would not matter. Drain thoroughly.

2. Put the lentils and water in a karahi, wok or saucepan, add to water and place over a high heat. Bring to the boil, and boil steadily for 8–10 minutes. Reduce the heat to low, cover and simmer for 30–35 minutes until the dhal is tender and has absorbed nearly all the water. The dhal at this stage should be rather like the consistency of baked beans. Remove from the heat and set aside.

3. Preheat a karahi or wok over medium heat for 1–2 minutes, then add the oil. When hot but not smoking, add the cassia or cinnamon and fennel seeds, and let them sizzle for 15–20 seconds, then add the garlic and stir-fry for 1 minute.

4. Add the crushed chillies followed by the onion and fresh chillies. Stir-fry for 2 minutes, add the salt, and stir-fry for a further 2–3 minutes.

5. Add the ground fennel, cumin and half the tomatoes. Stir-fry for 2–3 minutes or until you can see oil floating on the surface.

6. Add the cooked dhal, increase the heat slightly and stir-fry for 4–5 minutes. Add the remaining tomatoes, Kasoori methi, garam masala and remaining tomatoes. Stir-fry for 1 minute. Stir in the coriander leaves, remove from the heat and serve.

Preparation time: 30 minutes, plus soaking time for dhal

Cooking time: 15 minutes

Serving ideas: Serve with Balti Naan (pages 170–72) or Soda
   Naan (pages 178–80), accompanied by Gobi Andey (pages
   61–2) or Saag-Aloo (pages 66–8).

Suitable for freezing.

Dhal Panchrattan

(Five Types of Lentils)

Serves 4

This is a delicacy from the state of Punjab, using five types of lentils – 'panch' meaning five' and 'rattan' meaning 'jewels'. You can try other combinations too. Replace the whole moong dhal with urid dhal and channa dhal with tuvar dhal.

40g/1½oz masoor dhal (red split lentils)
40g/1½oz moong dhal (yellow split lentils)
40g/1½oz channa dhal or yellow split peas
40g/1½oz whole masoor dhal (whole brown lentils)
40g/1½oz whole moong dhal (mung beans)
900ml/1½ pints water
2 teaspoons ground cumin
1 teaspoon ground turmeric
2 x 2.5cm/1 inch pieces cassia bark or cinnamon sticks
1 teaspoon salt or to taste
50g/2oz ghee or unsalted butter
1 onion (about 175g/6oz), finely chopped
1–2 green chillies, seeded and cut into juliennes
2.5cm/½ inch cube root ginger, peeled and cut into juliennes
¼ teaspoon crushed dried chillies

117

75g/3oz canned chopped tomatoes including juice
½ teaspoon Balti Garam Masala (pages 28–9)
2 tablespoons chopped coriander leaves

1. Pick over each variety of lentils, mix together and wash in several changes of water. Soak them for 4–5 hours.
2. Put lentils and water in a karahi, wok or saucepan over a high heat. Bring to the boil and cook for 10 minutes, skimming off scum as necessary.
3. Add the cumin, turmeric and cassia or cinnamon, stir and reduce the heat to low. Cover (use a piece of foil if you are using a karahi) and simmer for 20–25 minutes, stirring occasionally. Stir in the salt and mash some of the lentils (about a quarter) with a spoon. Remove from the heat and set aside.
4. Preheat a karahi or wok over medium heat, and add the ghee or butter. When hot, stir-fry the onions, fresh chillies and ginger for 3–4 minutes, then add the dried chillies. Stir-fry for a further 30 seconds and add the tomatoes. Stir-fry for 2 minutes, then stir in the garam masala and coriander leaves. Add this mixture to the cooked dhal, stir well and return the pan to the heat. Let the dhal bubble for 1 minute, remove from the heat and serve.

Preparation time: 20–25 minutes, plus time to soak lentils
Cooking time: 45–50 minutes
Serving ideas: Serve with Balti Naan (pages 170–72) or Sada Chawal (pages 160–1).
Suitable for freezing.

Rajma Masala

□ V

(Spiced Red Kidney Beans)

Serves 4

Red kidney beans are wonderful to cook with spices. The dried beans are normally soaked and boiled until tender before being cooked. If you use dried beans, boil the beans for 10–15 minutes, drain, rinse and then cook them in fresh water. This process is necessary to remove the toxins present in red kidney beans. For an easy alternative, I have used canned beans for this recipe.

> 1 onion (about 175g/6oz), roughly chopped
> 2.5cm/1 inch cube root ginger, peeled and roughly chopped
> 4 cloves garlic, peeled and roughly chopped
> 4 tablespoons sunflower or corn oil
> 2 teaspoons ground cumin
> 2 teaspoons ground coriander
> ½ teaspoon ground turmeric
> ¼–½ teaspoon chilli powder
> 1 tablespoon tomato purée
> 625g/1lb canned red kidney beans, drained and rinsed
> 1 teaspoon salt or to taste

275ml/8 fl oz warm water
1 tablespoon Kasoori methi, dried stalks removed
3–4 green chillies (preferably the long slim ones)
½ teaspoon Balti Garam Masala (pages 28–9)
2 tablespoons chopped coriander leaves

1. Purée the onion, ginger and garlic in a food processor.
2. Preheat a karahi or wok over medium heat for 1–2 minutes, then add the oil. When hot, add the puréed ingredients and stir-fry for 4 minutes.
3. Reduce the heat to low, add the ground cumin and coriander, and stir-fry for 1 minute. Add the turmeric, chilli powder and tomato purée, and stir-fry for another minute.
4. Add the beans and salt, increase the heat to medium and stir-fry for 1 minute.
5. Add the water, Kasoori methi and chillies, then simmer gently for 5 minutes, stirring frequently.
6. Sprinkle with garam masala, stir in the coriander leaves, remove from the heat and serve.

Preparation time: 10 minutes
Cooking time: 15 minutes
Serving ideas: Serve with Methi ki Roti (pages 176–7) or Khumb Pulao (pages 164–5).
Variation: Use black-eyed beans or butter beans.
Suitable for freezing.

Tarka Dhal

(Lentils with Spicy Hot Oil Seasoning)

Serves 4

Pulses have been an important and essential food item in India where the vast majority of the population is vegetarian. Evidence of pulses being eaten even in ancient times has been traced in the remains of Indus Valley Civilization, the world's third literate society. The fertile and lush valley of the river Indus produces an abundance of crops for the inhabitants of Baltistan.

175g/6oz masoor dhal (red split lentils)
750ml/1¼ pints water
1 teaspoon ground turmeric
2 teaspoons ground cumin
1 teaspoon salt or to taste
40g/1½oz ghee or unsalted butter
4 cloves garlic, peeled and roughly chopped then crushed
1 onion (about 175g/6oz), finely chopped
¼–½ teaspoon crushed dried chillies
1 green chilli, seeded and cut into juliennes
2 small tomatoes, skinned and chopped (optional)
1 tablespoon chopped coriander leaves

1. Pick over and wash the dhal in several changes of water. Soak for 30 minutes, then drain well.

2. Put the dhal, water, turmeric and cumin into a karahi or saucepan over high heat, bring to the boil and cook for 3 minutes. Reduce the heat to low, partially cover the pan with a piece of foil or lid, and cook for 8–10 minutes or until it stops being frothy. Keep an eye on it, and add a little more water if necessary. Cover the pan fully and simmer for 20 minutes or until the lentils are tender and thick. At this stage, you can add more water if you find it too thick or dry. Stir in the salt and remove from heat.

3. Preheat a karahi or wok over medium heat for 1–2 minutes, then add the ghee or butter. When hot, add the garlic and stir-fry for 30 seconds or until lightly browned. Add the onion, increase the heat slightly and stir-fry for 3–4 minutes or until just beginning to colour.

4. Add the dried and fresh chillies and stir-fry for 30 seconds. Add the tomatoes (if used) and coriander leaves and stir-fry for 30 seconds. Pour this mixture over the cooked dhal, making sure you scrape off and add every bit of flavoured ghee and other ingredients in the karahi. Stir and mix thoroughly with the dhal.

Preparation time: 10 minutes, plus soaking the dhal
Cooking time: 35–40 minutes
Serving ideas: Serve with Balti Naan (pages 170–72) or Sada Chawal (pages 160–61) accompanied by Saag Aloo (pages 66–8) or Khumb-Aloo (pages 98–100).

Suitable for freezing.

Dhal Makhani
(*Lentils with Butter*)

Serves 4

This is probably the best known and best loved lentil delicacy in India, after Tarka Dhal. The lentils used here are whole brown lentils (whole masoor dhal). When skinned and split, they are known as red split lentils or masoor dhal. Whole masoor dhal is available in Asian stores and health food shops.

175g/6oz whole masoor dhal
2 tablespoons sunflower or corn oil
1 tablespoon tomato purée
10 cloves garlic, peeled and puréed
4cm/1½ inch cube root ginger, peeled and finely grated
1 teaspoon ground turmeric
1 teaspoon ground cumin
½ teaspoon chilli powder
600ml/1 pint hot water
2 tomatoes (about 150g/5oz), skinned and chopped
3–4 green chillies
1 teaspoon salt or to taste
40g/1½oz butter
200ml/7 fl oz single cream

123

2 teaspoons lime juice

2 tablespoons chopped coriander leaves

1. Pick over the lentils and wash in several changes of water. Soak for 3–4 hours or overnight if you wish. Drain well.
2. Preheat a karahi or wok over medium heat and add the oil. When hot, add the dhal and stir-fry for 2 minutes. Reduce the heat slightly and stir-fry for a further 2 minutes. Add the tomato purée, and stir-fry for 1 minute, then add the garlic, ginger, turmeric, ground cumin and chilli powder. Stir-fry for 2 minutes and add the water. Bring to the boil over a high heat and cook for 1 minute. Reduce the heat to low, cover the karahi or wok with a piece of foil or a lid, and simmer for 30–35 minutes, stirring half way through.
3. Mash about a quarter of the lentils with a wooden spoon. Add the tomatoes, chillies, salt, butter and cream, and cook gently for 5 minutes, uncovered.
4. Add the lime juice and coriander leaves, stir, remove from the heat and serve.

Preparation time: 15–20 minutes, plus soaking the lentils

Cooking time: 45 minutes

Serving ideas: Serve with Balti Naan (pages 170–72) accompanied by Gobi-Aloo-Saag (pages 144–5) or Aloo ki Bhaji (pages 84–5).

Suitable for freezing.

Moong Dhal Jhal Frazi

(Stir-fried Yellow Split Lentils)

Serves 4

Moong dhal is derived from skinned and split whole moong dhal (mung beans) and is available from health food stores, good supermarkets and Asian grocers. Jhal frazi, or stir-frying, is a wonderful way to cook moong dhal as it is probably the fastest cooking lentil.

175g/6oz moong dhal
50g/2oz ghee
3 x 2.5cm/1 inch pieces cassia bark or cinnamon sticks
4 green cardamom pods, split to the top of each pod
1cm/½ inch cube root ginger, peeled and cut into juliennes
1 large onion (about 225g/8oz), finely sliced
1–2 long slim dried red chillies, chopped
1 teaspoon salt or to taste
5–6 cloves garlic, peeled and crushed
1 teaspoon ground turmeric
2 teaspoons ground cumin
450ml/¾ pint warm water
100g/4oz canned chopped tomatoes including juice

4 green chillies

2 tablespoons chopped coriander leaves

1. Pick over the lentils and wash in several changes of water. Soak for 1–2 hours and drain.

2. Preheat a karahi or wok over medium heat for 1–2 minutes, then add the ghee. When the ghee has melted, add the cassia or cinnamon and cardamom pods, allow to sizzle for 15 seconds.

3. Add the ginger, stir-fry for 30 seconds, then add the onion, dried chillies and salt, and stir-fry for 4–5 minutes or until the onion begins to colour.

4. Add the garlic and turmeric and stir-fry for 30 seconds.

5. Drain the moong dhal and add with the ground cumin. Stir-fry for 2–3 minutes, then add 150ml/¼ pint of the water. Increase the heat to high and stir-fry until the water dries up. Add the remaining water, bring to the boil and reduce the heat to medium. Cook for 12–15 minutes, stirring frequently.

6. Add the tomatoes and fresh chillies, stir-fry for 5 minutes, then add the coriander. Stir-fry for 1 minute, remove from the heat and serve.

Preparation time: 10–15 minutes, plus soaking dhal

Cooking time: 30 minutes

Serving ideas: Serve with Peshawari Naan (pages 173–5) or Kaddu Malai (pages 86–8).

Adraki Moong Dhal

V

(Mung Beans with Ginger)

Serves 4

Mung beans are an excellent source of vitamin C. They are easily available from health food stores, supermarkets and, of course, Asian grocers. History has it that mung beans were used by the early Harrapan inhabitants around Baltistan. This particular dish is good enough to eat on its own as a snack. The beans can be cooked in advance if you wish, and kept in the fridge for up to 36 hours. They can also be frozen: simply thaw and proceed from step 3. You can utilize any left over in many delicious ways as you will see from the ideas given below.

175g/6oz whole moong dhal (mung beans)
300ml/½ pint water
2 tablespoons sunflower or corn oil
½ teaspoon black mustard seeds
½ teaspoon cumin seeds
1 teaspoon coriander seeds, pounded to a coarse texture
1 onion (about 175g/6oz), finely chopped
2.5cm/1 inch cube root ginger, peeled and cut into juliennes
1 green chilli, seeded and cut into juliennes

127

1 teaspoon salt or to taste

100g/4oz canned chopped tomatoes including juice

¼ teaspoon crushed dried chillies

½ teaspoon Balti Garam Masala (pages 28–9)

1. Pick over, wash and soak the mung beans overnight in plenty of cold water. Drain well.

2. Put the mung beans and water in a karahi, wok or a saucepan over a high heat. Bring to the boil, reduce the heat to medium, partially cover the pan and cook for 5–6 minutes. You will find that the beans will create quite a lot of froth when they are cooking. When the froth settles down, reduce the heat to low, cover and simmer for 15 minutes. The beans should be tender by this time and most of the water absorbed, leaving about 2 tablespoons. Remove the pan from the heat and set aside.

3. Preheat a karahi or wok over medium heat for 1–2 minutes, then add the oil. When hot but not smoking, add the mustard seeds. As soon as they pop, add the cumin and coriander. Stir-fry for 30 seconds and add the onion, ginger and fresh chilli. Increase the heat slightly and stir-fry for 4–5 minutes or until the onion is soft and beginning to colour slightly.

4. Add the cooked beans, along with any cooking liquid left in the pan, and salt. Stir-fry for 3–4 minutes, then add the tomatoes and crushed chillies. Stir-fry for 2 minutes.

5. Sprinkle with the garam masala, stir-fry for 1 minute, remove from the heat and serve.

Preparation time: 15 minutes, plus soaking the beans

Cooking time: 30 minutes

Serving ideas: Serve with Methi ki Roti (pages 176–7) or Sada
Chawal (pages 160–61) and Gobi Andey (pages 61–2).

What to do with leftovers: you can of course freeze any leftovers.
Alternatively, dress up the leftovers to give a completely
new look! Use it cold to make a lovely raita. Simply mix
mung beans with enough thick set whole milk natural
yogurt. You can also reheat and use it as a topping for
jacket potatoes and serve with a mixed salad.

Variation: Use canned butter beans, well drained and rinsed.

Palak Choley

V

(Spinach with Chickpeas)

Serves 4–6

The combination of spinach and chickpeas is visually pleasing as well as being rich in all the vitamins and nutrients. I have used fresh spinach but you can use frozen if you wish. Do make sure it is frozen leaf spinach and not the purée, and thaw and drain it first.

   1 large onion (about 225g/8oz), roughly chopped
   2.5cm/1 inch cube root ginger, peeled and roughly chopped
   1 long slim dried red chilli, chopped
   3 tablespoons sunflower or corn oil
   1 teaspoon fennel seeds
   6–8 cloves garlic, peeled and crushed
   1 tablespoon dhanna-jeera powder
   ½ teaspoon ground turmeric
   1 teaspoon paprika
   1 tablespoon tomato purée
   400g/14oz can chickpeas, drained and rinsed
   150ml/¼ pint warm water
   225g/8oz spinach, finely chopped
   1 teaspoon salt or to taste

130

100g/4oz canned chopped tomatoes including juice
½ teaspoon Balti Garam Masala (pages 28–9)

1. Purée the onion, ginger and red chilli in a food processor until smooth.
2. Preheat a karahi or wok over medium heat for 1–2 minutes, then add the oil. When hot but not smoking, add the fennel seeds followed by the garlic. Stir-fry for 30 seconds.
3. Add the dhanna-jeera powder, stir-fry for 30 seconds, then add the puréed ingredients. Stir-fry for 3 minutes or until the oil surfaces the spice paste.
4. Add the turmeric, paprika and tomato purée and stir-fry for 1 minute.
5. Add the chickpeas and water, bring to the boil then reduce the heat to low. Cover the karahi or wok with a lid or a piece of foil and simmer for 10 minutes.
6. Add the spinach and salt and increase the heat to medium-high. Stir-fry for 1 minute when the spinach will shrink and release its natural juices.
7. Add the tomatoes and stir-fry for 6–8 minutes, reducing the heat slightly if necessary. Sprinkle with the garam masala, stir-fry for 1 minute, then remove from the heat and serve.

Preparation time: 20–25 minutes
Cooking time: 25 minutes
Serving ideas: Serve with Soda Naan (pages 178–80) or Kashmir ki Roti (pages 168–9).
Suitable for freezing if fresh spinach is used.

Restaurant-Style
Recipes

Having visited many Balti restaurants, I am always struck by how the restaurateurs cope cheerfully in meeting the varying demands of their customers. I found them all very efficient and friendly.

A common feature of Balti restaurants is the 'combination dish' in which up to at least six vegetables are cooked together. Also, using a pre-prepared sauce and adding chosen ingredients to it is a common practice whether it is a Balti restaurant or traditional Indian one. Unlike home cooking, it is necessary for them to follow this practice in order to cope with the variety of dishes ordered.

Dhal-Aloo-Saag-Gajjar $\boxed{\text{V}}$

(Lentils with Potato, Spinach and Carrot)

Serves 4–6

Here is my own version of the various combination dishes that Balti restaurants in Birmingham seem to serve. I like the idea of a 'combination dish' because all the leftovers can be used to create an entirely new taste!

100g/4oz masoor dhal (red split lentils)
600ml/1 pint water
3 tablespoons sunflower or corn oil
3 cloves garlic, peeled and crushed
1cm/½ inch cube root ginger, peeled and grated
1 green chilli, seeded and chopped
1 small onion (about 100g/4oz), finely chopped
1 tablespoon dhanna-jeera powder
¼–½ teaspoon chilli powder
½ teaspoon Balti Garam Masala (pages 28–9)
½ teaspoon dried mint
225g/8oz spinach, finely chopped or frozen leaf spinach, thawed and chopped
175ml/6 fl oz Balti Base Sauce (pages 26–7)
100g/4oz carrots, peeled, cut into batons and parboiled

150g/5oz potatoes, boiled, peeled and cut into 2.5cm/
   1 inch cubes
1 teaspoon salt or to taste
2 tablespoons chopped coriander leaves

1. Pick over the lentils, wash in several changes of water and soak for 30 minutes (longer would not matter). Drain thoroughly.

2. Put the dhal and water in a karahi, wok or saucepan over a high heat and bring to the boil. Reduce the heat to low and partially cover the pan (if you are using a karahi, cover it with a piece of foil). At this stage, the lentils will be quite frothy, cook until the froth disappears, then cover the pan fully. Do not cover while any froth is present, as this will cause the liquid to spill over. Simmer for 30 minutes or until the lentils are tender and thick. Remove the pan from the heat and set aside.

3. Preheat a karahi or wok over medium heat and add the oil. When hot but not smoking, stir-fry the garlic, ginger and fresh chilli for 30 seconds. Add the onion, increase the heat slightly and stir-fry for 3–4 minutes or until just beginning to colour.

4. Add the dhanna-jeera powder, chilli powder, garam masala and mint, stir-fry for 30 seconds, then add the spinach. Stir-fry for 2–3 minutes or until the spinach has wilted and released its natural juices.

5. Add the base sauce and stir-fry for 2 minutes, then add the cooked dhal, carrots, potatoes and salt. Stir and mix thoroughly, bring to boiling point, then reduce the heat to

low and simmer for 2–3 minutes. Stir in the coriander leaves, remove from the heat and serve.

Preparation time: 30 minutes, plus time to soak the lentils
Cooking time: 45 minutes including pre-cooking lentils and vegetables
Serving ideas: Serve with Peshawari Naan (pages 173–5) and/or Sada Chawal (pages 160–61).

Kadhai (karahi) Sabziyon

(Balti Mixed Vegetables)

Serves 4–6

A quick and easy dish using parboiled vegetables. You can try any combination of vegetables you like; use the ones in this recipe as a guide.

> 3 tablespoons sunflower or corn oil
> 1 small onion, finely chopped
> 4 cloves garlic, peeled and crushed
> 1cm/½ inch cube root ginger, peeled and grated
> 1 tablespoon ground coriander
> 1 tablespoon ground cumin
> ¼–½ teaspoon chilli powder
> ½ teaspoon ground turmeric
> 1 tablespoon tomato purée
> 175ml/6 fl oz Balti Base Sauce (pages 26–7)
> 1 teaspoon Balti Garam Masala (pages 28–9)
> 275g/10oz old potatoes, boiled, peeled and cut into
>   2.5cm/1 inch cubes
> 150g/5oz green beans, trimmed, cut into 2.5cm/1 inch
>   pieces and parboiled
> 175g/6oz carrots, cut into batons and parboiled

175g/6oz cauliflower, divided into 2.5cm/1 inch florets
450ml/¾ pint warm water
1 teaspoon salt or to taste
2 tablespoons chopped coriander leaves

1. Preheat a karahi or wok over medium heat for 1–2 minutes, then add the oil. When hot, stir-fry the onion for 3–4 minutes.

2. Add the garlic, ginger, ground coriander and cumin, stir-fry for 1 minute, then add the chilli powder and turmeric. Stir-fry for 30 seconds and add the tomato purée. Stir-fry for 1 minute, and add the base sauce and garam masala. Stir-fry for 2–3 minutes, reducing the heat as the mixture gets drier and oil begins to surface the spice paste.

3. Add all the vegetables, water and salt. Bring to the boil, reduce the heat to low and simmer, uncovered, for 5 minutes. Stir in the coriander leaves, remove from the heat and serve.

Preparation time: 30–35 minutes

Cooking time: 15 minutes

Serving ideas: Serve with Balti Naan (pages 170–72) or Sada Chawal (pages 160–61) accompanied by Tarka Dhal (pages 121–2).

Suitable for freezing although the potato texture will change slightly.

Khumb-Aloo-Mattar-Makki [V]

(*Mushrooms, Potatoes, Peas and Sweetcorn*)

Serves 4–6

I first tasted a combination vegetable dish at the Royal Naim Balti Restaurant in Birmingham where about six different types of vegetables were used. When I asked the chef how he cooked so many vegetables, requiring different cooking time, to such perfection, he said they were all cooked separately and then mixed together. Here is an interesting combination for you using mushrooms (khumb), potatoes (aloo), garden peas (mattar) and sweetcorn (makki). I have, however, cooked them all together.

> 4 tablespoons sunflower or corn oil
> 1 small onion (about 100g/4oz), finely chopped
> 3 cloves garlic, peeled and crushed
> 2 teaspoons ground coriander
> 1 teaspoon ground cumin
> ¼–½ teaspoon chilli powder
> 1 tablespoon tomato purée
> 175ml/6 fl oz Balti Base Sauce (pages 26–7)
> 150g/5oz large flat mushrooms, cut into bite-sized pieces
> 75g/3oz frozen garden peas, thawed, or cooked fresh peas

141

75g/3oz frozen sweetcorn, thawed, or canned
   sweetcorn, drained and rinsed
300g/11oz old potatoes, boiled, peeled and cut into
2.5cm/1 inch cubes
300ml/½ pint warm water
1 teaspoon salt or to taste
½ teaspoon dried mint
¼ teaspoon Balti Garam Masala (pages 28–9)
2 tablespoons chopped coriander leaves

1. Preheat a karahi or wok over medium heat for 1–2
   minutes, then add the oil. When hot, stir-fry the onion for
   3–4 minutes, add the garlic, ground coriander, cumin and
   chilli powder, and stir-fry for 1 minute.
2. Add the tomato purée and base sauce, and stir-fry for 2–3
   minutes, reducing the heat to low as it begins to dry up
   and oil starts floating on the surface.
3. Add the mushrooms, peas, corn and potatoes, stir-fry for
   2 minutes and add the water, salt and mint. Bring to the
   boil, cover with a lid or a piece of foil, and reduce the heat
   to low. Simmer for 8–10 minutes.
4. Stir in the garam masala and coriander leaves, remove
   from the heat and serve.

Preparation time: 15 minutes
Cooking time: 20 minutes
Serving ideas: Serve with Balti Naan (pages 170–72) or Soda
   Naan (pages 178–80) accompanied by Dhal Makhani
   (pages 123–4).

What to do with leftovers: Lightly mash the vegetables and reheat briefly, if necessary, to obtain a drier consistency. Make croquettes, roll in plain flour, dip in beaten egg and roll in breadcrumbs. Deep fry until golden brown.

Gobi-Aloo-Saag

V

(Cauliflower, Potatoes and Spinach)

Serves 4–6

The Balti restaurants in Birmingham have an amazing range of 'combination' dishes. They combine just about anything to create one dish and often mix individual portions of several cooked dishes to concoct a very interesting and delicious dish. Here is a simple combination which tastes wonderful.

> 2 tablespoons sunflower or corn oil
> ½ teaspoon black mustard seeds
> ½ teaspoon cumin seeds
> ¼ teaspoon fenugreek seeds
> 6–8 curry leaves (optional)
> 4 cloves garlic, peeled and crushed
> 1 teaspoon ground cumin
> 1½ teaspoons ground coriander
> ½ teaspoon chilli powder
> ½ teaspoon ground turmeric
> 225g/8oz spinach, finely chopped
> 75ml/3 fl oz Balti Base Sauce (pages 26–7)
> 225g/8oz parboiled cauliflower
> 150g/5oz chopped canned tomatoes including juice

225g/8oz potatoes, boiled, peeled and cut into 2.5cm/
  1 inch cubes
1 teaspoon salt or to taste
½ teaspoon Balti Garam Masala (pages 28–9)

1. Preheat a karahi or wok over medium heat for 1–2
   minutes, then add the oil. When quite hot but not
   smoking, add the mustard seeds. As soon as they pop, add
   the cumin, fenugreek and curry leaves (if used). Stir-fry
   for 15 seconds.
2. Add the garlic and stir-fry until just beginning to colour,
   then add the ground cumin, coriander, chilli powder and
   turmeric. Stir-fry for 30 seconds.
3. Add the spinach, increase heat slightly and stir-fry for 2–3
   minutes or until the spinach wilts and starts to release its
   natural juices. Add 2 tablespoons of the base sauce and
   stir-fry for 1 minute.
4. Add the cauliflower, tomatoes and potatoes, and stir-fry
   for 2 minutes. Add the remaining base sauce, salt and
   garam masala, stir-fry for 2 minutes, remove from the
   heat and serve.

Preparation time: 25–30 minutes, excluding time needed for
  base sauce
Cooking time: 12–15 minutes
Serving ideas: Serve with Soda Naan (pages 178–80) or Balti
  Naan (pages 170–72) and a protein-rich dish such as Tarka
  Dhal (pages 121–2).
Not suitable for freezing.

Aloo-Choley

(Potatoes with Chick Peas)

Serves 4–6

A well-known delicacy from the state of Punjab in Northern India, Aloo-Choley is very popular all over India. You can use dried chick peas which you will need to soak overnight and cook before adding to the spices. Alternatively, use canned chick peas which are ready to use and work extremely well.

3 tablespoons sunflower or corn oil
2.5cm/1 inch cube root ginger, peeled and cut into juliennes
1–2 green chillies, seeded and cut into juliennes
6 cloves garlic, peeled and pounded to a pulp
1 onion (about 175g/6oz), finely sliced
1 teaspoon salt or to taste
1 tablespoon dhanna-jeera powder
½ teaspoon ground turmeric
¼–½ teaspoon chilli powder
100g/4oz passata or canned tomatoes with juice, sieved
400g/14oz can chick peas, drained and well rinsed
150ml/¼ pint Balti Base Sauce (pages 26–7)

150ml/¼ pint warm water

175g/6oz boiled potatoes, peeled and cut into 2.5cm/
    1 inch cubes

40g/1½oz red pepper, seeded and cubed (optional)

40g/1½oz green pepper, seeded and cubed (optional)

1 tablespoon Kasoori methi, dried stalks removed

2 tablespoons chopped coriander leaves

1. Preheat a karahi or wok over medium heat for 1–2 minutes. Add the oil, and when hot but not smoking, add the ginger, fresh chillies and garlic. Stir-fry for 30 seconds.

2. Add the onion and salt and increase the heat slightly. Stir-fry for 4–5 minutes or until the onion is soft and just beginning to colour.

3. Add the dhanna-jeera powder, turmeric and chilli powder, and stir-fry for 1 minute. Add the passata or sieved tomatoes, and stir-fry for 2 minutes.

4. Add the chick peas, base sauce and water, bring to the boil and reduce the heat to low. Cover the karahi or wok with a lid or a piece of foil and simmer for 10 minutes.

5. Add the potatoes, peppers (if used) and kasoori methi, then cook until the potatoes are heated through (about 5 minutes).

6. Stir in the coriander leaves, remove from the heat and serve.

Preparation time: 20–25 minutes

Cooking time: 20 minutes

147

Serving ideas: Serve with Balti Naan (pages 170–72) or
   Peshawari Naan (pages 173–5).

Suitable for freezing if frozen before adding potatoes. Defrost
   thoroughly before reheating. Reheat in a preheated karahi
   or wok, adding a little warm water if necessary.

Aloo Mattar

V

(Potatoes with Garden Peas)

Serves 4

Many people do not associate peas with Indian cooking. But, as you will have realised from the recipes in this book, peas are very popular in India. Aloo Mattar is a well-known dish from Northern India.

3 tablespoons sunflower or corn oil
1 small onion, finely chopped
2 cloves garlic, peeled and crushed
5mm/¼ inch cube root ginger, finely grated
2 teaspoons ground cumin
2 teaspoons ground coriander
¼ teaspoon ground turmeric
¼–½ teaspoon chilli powder
1 tablespoon tomato purée
½ teaspoon dried mint
450g/1lb old potatoes, boiled peeled and cut into
2.5cm/1 inch cubes
100g/4oz frozen garden peas or cooked fresh peas
300ml/½ pint Balti Base Sauce (pages 26–7)
1 teaspoon salt or to taste

149

½ teaspoon Balti Garam Masala (pages 28–9)

2 tablespoons chopped coriander leaves

1. Preheat a karahi or wok over medium heat for 1–2 minutes, then add the oil. When hot, stir-fry the onion for 3–4 minutes or until starting to colour.
2. Add the garlic and ginger, and stir-fry for 30 seconds. Add the cumin, coriander, turmeric and chilli powder. Stir-fry for 1 minute, add the tomato purée and mint, and stir-fry for 1 minute.
3. Add the potatoes, peas, base sauce and salt, bring to a slow simmer and cook for 5–6 minutes. Stir in the garam masala and coriander leaves and cook for 1 minute. Remove from the heat and serve.

Preparation time: 20–25 minutes

Cooking time: 12–15 minutes

Serving ideas: Serve with Balti Naan (pages 170–72) and Tarka Dhal (pages 121–2) or Palak Choley (page 130–31) or Rajma Masala (pages 119–20).

Kashmiri Sabziyon

V

(Kashmiri Vegetables)

Serves 4

When I visited the 'I am the King of Balti' restaurant in Birmingham, I asked the Kashmiri chef to show me a special vegetable dish. He very willingly demonstrated the following recipe. Here is my version, using the same vegetable combination.

3 tablespoons sunflower or soya oil

3–4 cloves garlic, peeled and crushed

1cm/½ inch cube root ginger, peeled and finely grated

1½ teaspoons ground coriander

1 teaspoon ground cumin

½ teaspoon ground turmeric

½ teaspoon chilli powder

175g/6oz closed cup mushrooms, sliced

450ml/¾ pint Balti Base Sauce (pages 26–7)

150g/5oz frozen sweetcorn, thawed, or canned
    sweetcorn, drained and rinsed

175g/6oz canned unsweetened pineapple cubes, drained

50g/2oz glacé cherries, halved and rinsed

¼ teaspoon Balti Garam Masala (pages 28–9)

1 tablespoon chopped coriander leaves

151

1. Preheat a karahi or wok over medium heat and add the oil. When hot, stir-fry the garlic and ginger for 30 seconds, reduce the heat slightly and add the ground coriander, cumin, turmeric and chilli powder. Stir-fry for 30 seconds and add the mushrooms. Stir-fry for 1–2 minutes.

2. Add the base sauce and cook until the sauce is heated through. Add the sweetcorn, pineapple and cherries. Simmer, uncovered, for 5 minutes. Stir in the garam masala and coriander leaves, remove from the heat and serve.

Preparation time: 15 minutes

Cooking time: 12-15 minutes

Serving ideas: Serve with Kashmir ki Roti (pages 168–9) and Dhal Panchrattan (pages 117–18).

Aloo-Gobi-Dhal-Baigan $\boxed{\text{V}}$

(Potato, Cauliflower, Lentils and Aubergine)

Serves 4–6

Preparing and cooking aubergines can be slightly tricky. I have, therefore, included instructions to make this easy. The other vegetables can be pre-cooked in any way you find convenient.

75g/3oz masoor dhal (red split lentils)
300ml/½ pint water
1 aubergine (about 175g/6oz)
4 tablespoons sunflower or corn oil
1 small onion (about 100g/4oz), finely chopped
1cm/½ inch cube root ginger, peeled and grated
3–4 cloves garlic, peeled and crushed
1 teaspoon ground coriander
1 teaspoon ground cumin
½ teaspoon chilli powder
300ml/½ pint Balti Base Sauce (pages 26–7)
175g/6oz cauliflower, divided into 2.5cm/1 inch florets
    and parboiled
200g/7oz potatoes, boiled, peeled and cut into
    2.5cm/1 inch cubes

153

1 teaspoon salt or to taste

½ teaspoon Balti Garam Masala (pages 28–9)

2 tablespoons chopped coriander leaves

1. Pick over the lentils, wash and soak for 30 minutes – longer would not matter.

2. Drain the lentils thoroughly. Put in a karahi, wok or saucepan, add the water and bring to the boil over high heat. Reduce the heat to medium, partially cover the pan and cook for 8–10 minutes or until it stops being frothy. Now cover the pan fully, reduce the heat to low, and simmer for 20–25 minutes or until the lentils are tender and thick. Remove from the heat and set aside.

3. Cut the aubergine into bite-sized pieces and soak in salted water for 30 minutes. Drain and rinse. Put the aubergine in a panful of boiling water and boil, covered, for 5 minutes. When you first put the aubergine in the pan, it will float. After a few minutes, when it has soaked up some water, it will sink. Once it has sunk, it will cook fast and you will overcook it if you do not watch out! Boil for 2–3 minutes and drain, then rinse in cold water to prevent further cooking.

4. Preheat a karahi or wok over medium heat and add the oil. When hot, stir-fry the onion for 3–4 minutes, then add the ginger, garlic, coriander, cumin and chilli powder. Stir-fry for 1 minute and add the cooked dhal. Stir-fry for 1 minute.

5. Add the base sauce, all the cooked vegetables, salt and garam masala. Bring to the boil, reduce the heat to low

and simmer, uncovered, for 3–4 minutes. Stir in the coriander leaves, remove from the heat and serve.

Preparation time: 30–35 minutes, plus soaking time for lentils and aubergines. This includes pre-cooking time for potatoes and cauliflower
Cooking time: 20–25 minutes
Serving ideas: Serve with Peshawari Naan (pages 173–5) or Soda Naan (pages 178–80).

Rice and Bread

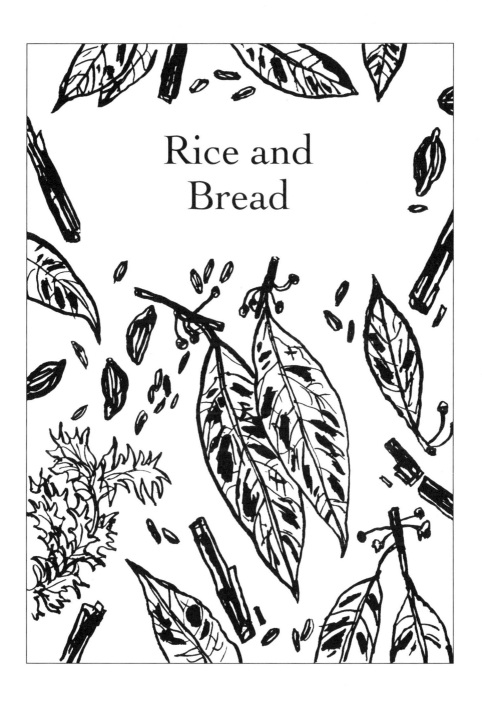

In this chapter, I have provided a wider choice of bread rather than restrict you to the 'Balti Naan'. All of these can be made ahead of time and frozen, so you can serve a selection of breads if you wish. You can also combine bread and rice as is done for traditional Indian meals. To make your Balti meals varied, interesting and more balanced, I have included a small selection of rice recipes. Details of preparing and cooking rice can be found on page 14. Rice provides protein, vitamins and minerals and you will have plenty of dietary fibre from the bread. We all know how important fibre is in reducing blood cholesterol.

Sada Chawal

(Plain Boiled Basmati Rice)

Serves 4–6

The wonderful natural aroma and flavour of basmati rice seems to have the power to complement any accompanying dish. In India, basmati is known as 'the king of rice'; it receives a special treatment which no other rice does. Unlike other long-grain rice, basmati is not packed for the market just after it is harvested. It is matured for two to four years before it is ready for commercial purposes. It is during this maturing time that the rice develops that wonderful, distinctive flavour, a bit like good wine! Please read the instructions for preparing and cooking rice before you try this or any other rice recipe in this chapter.

> 275g/10oz basmati rice
> 550ml/18 fl oz water
> ½ teaspoon salt
> knob of butter

1. Wash the rice in several changes of water and soak for 30 minutes. Drain thoroughly.

2. Put the water in a karahi, wok or saucepan and bring to

the boil over high heat. Add the rice, salt and butter, bring back to the boil and cook for 1 minute. Reduce the heat to low and cover the pan tightly (if using karahi use a piece of foil to cover). Cook for 10 minutes without lifting the lid. Remove from the heat and set aside, undisturbed, for 10–15 minutes.

3. Fork through the rice, and using a flat metal or plastic spoon, transfer it to a serving dish.

Preparation time: A few minutes, plus soaking the rice
Cooking time: 15 minutes
Serving ideas: Serve with any Balti dish.

Kesari Chawal

(Saffron Rice)

Serves 4–6

The best varieties of saffron come from India (Kashmir) and La Mancha in Spain.

275g/10oz basmati rice
600ml/1 pint water
3 x 2.5cm/1 inch pieces cassia bark or cinnamon sticks
6 whole cloves
6 green cardamom, split to the top of each pod
½ teaspoon black peppercorns
2 bay leaves crumbled
1 teaspoon salt
½ teaspoon saffron strands, pounded
2 tablespoons hot milk
50g/2oz ghee or unsalted butter
1 large onion (about 250g/8oz), finely sliced

To garnish
15g/½oz toasted flaked almonds
few sprigs of fresh coriander

1. Wash the rice in several changes of water and soak for 30 minutes. Drain well.

2. Put the water, cassia or cinnamon, cloves, cardamom, peppercorns, bay leaves and salt into a saucepan. Bring to the boil, cover and simmer for 15 minutes. Strain and set aside.

3. Soak the saffron in the hot milk and set aside for 10–15 minutes.

4. Melt the ghee over medium heat in a karahi, wok or saucepan. Add the fry onion and stir-fry until a pale golden colour, about 9–10 minutes. Add the rice, reduce the heat to low and stir-fry for 2–3 minutes.

5. Add the spiced liquid and saffron milk with all the strands and increase the heat to high. Bring to the boil, cover the pan (if using karahi, use a piece of foil to cover) and reduce the heat to very low. Cook for 10 minutes. Remove from the heat and leave undisturbed for 10–15 minutes.

6. Fork through the rice, then using a flat plastic or metal spoon, transfer to a serving dish. Serve garnished with toasted almonds and sprigs of coriander.

Preparation time: 15 minutes, plus soaking the rice
Cooking time: 25–30 minutes
Serving ideas: Serve with Paneer Kofta Makhani (pages 58–60) and a raita.
Suitable for freezing.

Khumb Pulao

(Mushroom Pulao)

Serves 4–6

Balti food is traditionally eaten with naan, perhaps because rice was not known to the early settlers. Wheat and barley were the staples during those days. In keeping with this tradition, current cuisine also consists of more wheat than rice. However, now that we have the exquisite basmati rice, which grows in abundance in the foothills of the Himalayas, why not combine both naan and rice to make your Balti meals more interesting and varied? You will be delighted with this Mushroom Pulao.

275g/10oz basmati rice
50g/2oz ghee or unsalted butter
4 green cardamom pods, split to the top of each pod
3 x 2.5cm/1 inch pieces cassia bark or cinnamon sticks
2 bay leaves, crumbled
4 cloves garlic, peeled and crushed
4 whole cloves
1 large onion (about 225g/8oz), finely sliced
1 green chilli, seeded and chopped
1 teaspoon Balti Garam Masala (pages 28–9)
75g/3oz canned chopped tomatoes including juice

164

225g/8oz large flat mushrooms, cut into chunky pieces
2 tablespoons chopped coriander leaves
1 teaspoon salt or to taste
550ml/18 fl oz warm water

1. Wash the rice in several changes of water and soak for 30 minutes. Drain and set aside.

2. Preheat a karahi, wok or a heavy-based saucepan over medium heat, then add the ghee or butter. When hot but not smoking, reduce the heat slightly and add the cardamom, cassia and bay leaves, and let them sizzle for 15–20 seconds.

3. Add the garlic and cloves, and stir-fry for 30 seconds, then add the onion and chilli. Increase the heat to medium-high and stir-fry for 4–5 minutes.

4. Add the garam masala and stir-fry for 30 seconds. Add the tomatoes and stir-fry for 1 minute.

5. Add the rice, mushrooms, coriander leaves and salt, stir-fry for 1 minute, then add the water. Bring to the boil, and cook for 1 minute. Reduce the heat to low, cover the pan with a piece of foil or a lid and cook for 10 minutes. Remove from the heat and leave to stand undisturbed for 5–6 minutes. Remove the whole spices if desired, and fork through the pulao before serving.

Preparation time: 20 minutes, plus soaking the rice
Cooking time: 25 minutes
Serving ideas: Serve with Tarka Dhal (pages 121–2) and a Raita.
Suitable for freezing.

165

Kashmiri Sabzi Pulao

(Kashmiri Vegetable Pulao)

Serves 4

A few centuries ago, the 'Naga' tribes of Kashmir were ruled by Kashya, a good and benevolent leader. As a tribute to him, his people named this land 'Kashya-Mor' which means 'Abode of the descendants of Kashya'. 'Kashya-Mor' became 'Kashmir'. The 'Sarawat' tribes eventually forced the Nagas to migrate from this region.

Kashmir is renowned for its exotic fruits and vegetables which the local people have used very imaginatively to create wonderful dishes.

175g/6oz large flat mushrooms
40g/1½oz ghee or unsalted butter
1 onion (about 175g/6oz), finely sliced
4 x 2.5cm/1 inch cassia bark or cinnamon sticks
4 whole cloves
4 green cardamom pods, split to the top of each pod
2 bay leaves, crumbled
50g/2oz dried, ready-to-eat apricot, sliced
75g/3oz canned pineapple cubes, well drained
50g/2oz glacé cherries, halved and rinsed

225g/8oz basmati rice, washed, soaked in cold water for
    30 minutes, well drained
1 teaspoon salt or to taste
½ teaspoon chilli powder
475ml/16 fl oz warm water
1 tablespoon chopped coriander leaves

1. Quarter the mushrooms and halve each quarter.
2. Preheat a karahi or wok over medium heat for 1–2
   minutes. Add the ghee or butter, and when hot but
   not smoking, add the onion, cassia or cinnamon, cloves,
   cardamom and bay leaves. Stir-fry for 3–4 minutes.
3. Add the mushrooms and stir-fry for 2 minutes.
4. Add all the fruits, with the rice, salt and chilli powder, and
   stir-fry for 2–3 minutes.
5. Add the water, bring to the boil and cook for 5 minutes.
   Add the coriander leaves and stir well.
6. Reduce the heat to very low, cover the pan with a lid or a
   piece of foil and cook for 6–7 minutes. Remove from the
   heat and leave to rest for 5–7 minutes. Use a metal or thin
   plastic spatula to stir and serve the rice, a wooden spoon
   will squash the grains.

Preparation time: 10–15 minutes, plus soaking the rice
Cooking time: 25 minutes
Serving ideas: Serve with Dhal Makhani (pages 123–4) and
    Tamatar aur Khira ka Raita (pages 189–90).
Suitable for freezing.

Kashmir ki Roti

(Kashmiri Bread)

Makes 8

Barley and wheat have been staple foods of the Baltistanis since the Harappan times. Archaeological findings include brick built objects with remains of wooden pestles to grind wheat into flour. Kashmiris still follow this practice today. The modern day tava (iron griddle) for cooking bread, must have been refined to its present state from clay and metal plate models found in the Indus Valley sites.

> 450g/1lb atta or chapatti flour
> 1 teaspoon salt
> 2 teaspoons sugar
> 1 teaspoon shahi jeera (royal cumin)
> 1 teaspoon onion seeds (kalonji)
> 275ml/8 fl oz warm milk
> 50g/2oz ghee or unsalted butter, melted
> Oil for shallow frying

1. Put the flour, salt, sugar, shahi jeera and kalonji in a large mixing bowl and mix thoroughly.

2. Gradually add the warm milk and knead until a dough is

formed. Alternatively, use a food processor with a dough hook. For both methods, now add the melted ghee or butter and knead for 2–3 minutes or until the fat is absorbed by the dough. If using a food processor, knead the dough until it stops sticking to the bowl and dough hook. For the hand method, transfer the dough to a pastry board and knead until it is soft and pliable and stops sticking to the board. Divide the dough into 2 equal parts and make 4 equal portions out of each. Rotate each portion between your palms to make a ball, then flatten by pressing down. Cover the flattened cakes with a damp cloth and set aside for 20 minutes.

3. Preheat a cast iron griddle or other heavy-based frying pan over medium heat. Roll out a flattened cake to a 20.5cm/8 inch round disc and place on the griddle. Allow to cook for 1 minute, turn over and cook the other side for 1 minute. Meanwhile, spread a little oil (about 1 tea-spoon) on the cooked side, turn over and spread oil on the second cooked side. Cook the first oiled side until brown patches appear; you can check this by lifting the roti gently. Turn it over and cook the second oiled side.

4. Place the cooked roti on one end of a long piece of foil lined with absorbent paper. Cover with the other end to keep hot while you cook the remaining rotis.

Preparation time: 15–20 minutes
Cooking time: 20–25 minutes
Serving ideas: Serve with Moong Dhal Jhal Frazi (pages 76–7).
Suitable for freezing.

169

Balti Naan

Makes 3

Kabul, the capital of Afghanistan, boasts the greatest and the best variety of naans. It must have been from Afghanistan that the Pathans first took naan to the North West Frontier Province. Balti Naan is fun to make and is great with all Balti dishes. There is nothing really different about Balti Naan except its size. It can be as long as 45.5cm/18 inches and as wide as 25.5cm/10 inches! Perhaps this was to facilitate the communal eating habits of the Baltistanis. A large naan enabled everyone to reach it from all corners of the table!

450g/1lb plain flour
1½ teaspoons baking powder
1 teaspoon salt
1 tablespoon sugar
1 teaspoon onion seeds (kalonji)
1 teaspoon shahi jeera (royal cumin)
50g/2oz ghee or unsalted butter, melted
275ml/8 fl oz warm milk
40g/1½oz natural yogurt

1. Put the flour, baking powder, salt, sugar, onion seeds and shahi jeera in a large mixing bowl and mix well. Add the ghee or butter and work it in with your fingertips. Alternatively, use a food processor with a dough hook and mix for a few seconds. The next step applies to both methods.

2. Gradually add the milk and mix until a soft dough is formed. For the hand method, transfer the dough to a pastry board and knead for 3–4 minutes until the dough is soft and smooth and does not stick to your fingers any more. If using a food processor, run it until all the milk is absorbed, then stop the processor and feel the dough. The dough hook and sides of the bowl should be clean, and the dough should feel soft and smooth. Put the dough in a plastic food bag or cover it well, and allow to rest for 1–1½ hours.

3. Preheat the oven to 220°C/425°F/gas mark 7. Preheat a large baking sheet and place greased greaseproof paper or baking parchment on top.

4. Use a large pastry board or flat surface to roll out the naan. Grease the board and the rolling pin lightly. Divide the dough into 3 equal parts, then make a smooth round ball. Flatten the ball and roll out to a 20cm/8 inch disc. Gently pull the lower end to form a teardrop shape, and roll again to make it about 40.5cm/16 inches long, maintaining the teardrop shape. The widest part can be about 23cm/9 inches and the narrowest 10cm/4 inches.

5. It is not necessary for you to make the naan into a teardrop shape. You can make them round or square if

171

you like. This traditional shape is due the fact that naan is hung onto the wall of the tandoor, the Indian clay oven. Gravity causes the naan to stretch, thus forming a tear-drop shape.

6. Place the naan on the prepared baking sheet and brush generously with the natural yogurt. Bake on the top shelf of the oven for 8–9 minutes. Until you finish baking all 3 naan, keep baked ones warm by wrapping in foil lined with absorbent paper.

Preparation time: 10–15 minutes, plus resting the dough
Cooking time: 25–28 minutes
Serving ideas: Serve with any Balti dish.
Suitable for freezing.

Peshawari Naan

Makes 6

Peshawar, in the North West Frontier Province close to the Khyber Pass, is a 'Pathan' stronghold. The Pathans, believed to be originally from Israel, made their first home in Afghanistan. It was here that they were converted to Islam. Today they are found living in various towns and cities in northern India and Pakistan. Peshawari Naan needs no introduction! It must be the most popular bread that forms part of most Indian restaurant menus. Here is my version.

450g/1lb plain flour
1 teaspoon baking powder
1 teaspoon salt
1 tablespoon sugar
1 dessertspoon easy-blend yeast
160g/5½oz ghee or unsalted butter, melted
290ml/9 fl oz warm milk
15g/½oz seedless raisins, coarsely chopped
25g/1oz flaked almonds, lightly crushed
little extra flour for dusting
1 tablespoon natural yogurt
1 tablespoon white poppy seeds or sesame seeds

173

1. Put the flour, baking powder, salt, sugar and yeast in a large warmed mixing bowl and mix thoroughly. Add half the melted ghee or butter and mix well. Gradually add the warm milk and mix into a stiff dough. Alternatively, use a food processor with a dough hook.

2. For both methods, now add the remaining melted ghee or butter and knead for 2–3 minutes for the hand method, and 50–60 seconds in the food processor. The dough will be very sticky at this stage – do not panic!

3. For the hand method, transfer the dough onto a pastry board, add the raisins and almonds, and knead until it stops sticking to the board and your fingers. Make sure the raisins and almonds are well distributed. If using a food processor, add the raisins and nuts and run it until the bowl and the dough hook are clean.

4. Put the dough in a large plastic bag and tie securely, leaving room for expansion. Put the bag in a warmed bowl, preferably a steel one as it will retain the heat better. If you do not have one, use a saucepan. Leave in a warm place (the airing cupboard is ideal) for 1–1½ hours to prove.

5. Divide the dough into 2 parts and make 3 equal portions from each. Rotate each portion between your palms, and press gently to flatten it into a round cake. Cover the flattened cakes and keep aside for 10 minutes. Preheat the oven to 220°C/425°F/gas mark 7.

6. Lightly dust each cake in flour and roll out to a 15cm/6 inch disc. Place one hand on the top end of the disc and gently pull the lower end to form a teardrop shape. This

shape is not absolutely necessary. You can make your naan round or even square if you like!

7. Preheat a baking sheet and place greased greaseproof paper or baking parchment on top. Put 2–3 naans on the baking sheet (depending on size), and brush the tops with a little yogurt. Sprinkle with poppy or sesame seeds and bake on the top shelf of the oven for 8–9 minutes or until puffed and lightly browned.

Preparation time: 15–20 minutes, plus proving the dough

Cooking time: 18–20 minutes

Serving ideas: Serve with Aloo Choley (pages 146–8) or Kadhai (karahi) Sabziyon (pages 139–40).

Suitable for freezing.

Methi ki Roti

$\boxed{\text{V}}$

(Fenugreek-flavoured Bread)

Makes 8

Kasoori methi (dried fenugreek leaves) is an ingredient that gives Balti dishes their characteristic flavour. It grows abundantly in Kasoor, in Pakistan – hence the name Kasoori methi – and is considered to be the best. The fresh leaves are dried and chopped with their stalks, which you need to remove. They come in packets and are available in Asian stores.

  450g/1lb atta or chappati flour
  1 teaspoon salt
  2 teaspoons sugar
  2 tablespoons Kasoori methi, stalks removed
  2–3 cloves garlic, peeled and crushed
  75ml/3 fl oz sunflower or corn oil
  290ml/9 fl oz warm water
  extra flour for dusting
  Sunflower or corn oil for frying

1. Put the flour in a large mixing bowl. Add the salt, sugar, Kasoori methi and garlic, and mix thoroughly with your fingertips.

2. Add the oil and work it well into the flour. Gradually add the warm water and knead until you have a soft dough. Transfer the dough to a pastry board and knead with your hands until the dough is soft and smooth and does not stick to your fingers or the board. Alternatively, make the dough in a food processor, kneading the dough until it has stopped sticking to the dough hook and bowl. Now cover the dough with a damp cloth and leave to rest for 20–30 minutes.

3. Divide the dough into 2 equal parts and either break off or cut 4 equal portions from each. Flatten each portion by rotating it between your palms and pressing it down to a flat cake. Cover again with a damp cloth. Preheat a cast iron griddle or other heavy-based frying pan over a medium heat for 2–3 minutes.

4. Dust one flat cake in flour and roll out to an 18cm/7 inch disc. Carefully lift from the board and place on the griddle. Cook for 1 minute, then turn over and cook the other side for 30–40 seconds. Meanwhile, spread the entire surface of the side you cooked first, with 1 teaspoon oil. Turn over the roti and cook until brown patches appear (you can lift it to check this, using a thin flat spatula). Now oil the second side, turn over and cook. Each roti will take 2–3 minutes. Transfer the cooked rotis to a plate lined with absorbent paper.

Preparation time: 15–20 minutes
Cooking time: 25 minutes
Serving ideas: Serve with Makki Khumb Jhal Frazi (pages 106–107) and Rajma Masala (pages 119–20).
Suitable for freezing.

Soda Naan

Makes 6

'Naan' is a Persian word which simply means 'bread'. The Persians, having entered India through the Khyber Pass, first settled in Kashmir. Originally a predominantly Hindu state, it now has a staggering 90 per cent Muslim population. Clay ovens, looking remarkably like the tandoor in which naan is baked, have been found by archaeologists in the Indus Valley Sites.

I offer you this plain naan for which I use soda water in the dough, a tip given by an aunt. This makes the naan wonderfully soft and fluffy: it literally melts in the mouth!

450g/1lb self-raising flour or plain flour with ½
    teaspoon baking powder
1 teaspoon salt
1 teaspoon sugar
1 dessertspoon easy-blend yeast
65g/2½oz ghee or unsalted butter, melted
300–350ml/10–12 fl oz soda water

1. Put the flour, salt, sugar and yeast into a warmed bowl and mix thoroughly. (It is best to use flour which

is already at warm room temperature.)

2. Make sure the ghee or butter is lukewarm, reserve 1 tablespoon and work the remainder into the flour with your fingertips.

3. Gradually add the soda water and mix until you have a fairly sticky dough. You can make the dough in a food processor with a dough hook if you wish. When the dough is formed, add the reserved fat and knead until the dough does not stick to the bowl or the dough hook.

4. For the hand-mixed method, transfer the dough to a pastry board and knead with your hands for 2–3 minutes. Add the remaining ghee or butter, and knead until the dough stops sticking to your fingers and the board.

5. Put the dough into a large plastic food bag and tie loosely. Place the bag in a warmed metal or steel bowl, or if you do not have one, use a saucepan. Leave the dough in a warm place for 45–50 minutes.

6. Knock back the dough and divide into 4 equal portions, cover and leave to rise again for 15–20 minutes.

7. Preheat oven to 220°C/425°F/gas mark 7. Place greased greaseproof paper or baking parchment on top of a baking sheet.

8. Use a large pastry board or flat surface to roll out the naan. Lightly grease your palms with a little oil then grease a portion of dough by patting and tossing it from one palm to another. Roll out to a 15cm/6 inch disc, and gently pull one end to form a teardrop shape. The shape of the naan is not important. You can make them round or square if you like!

179

9. Bake on the top shelf of the oven for 8–9 minutes.

Preparation time: 15–20 minutes, plus proving the dough
Cooking time: 18–20 minutes
Serving ideas: Serve with any Balti meal.

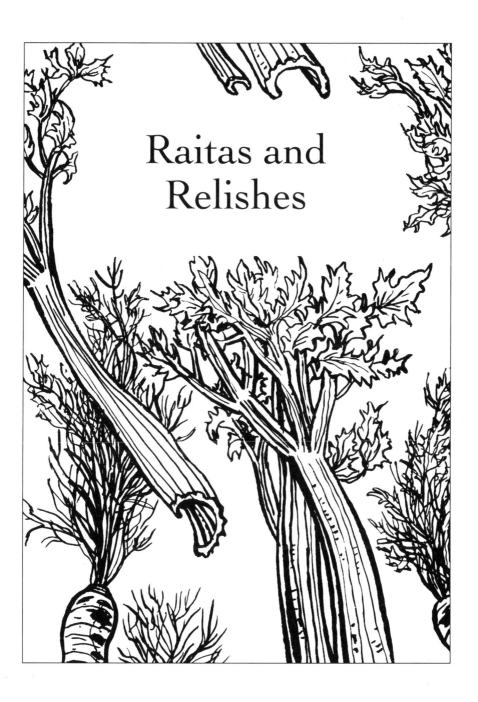

Raitas and
Relishes

Raitas and relishes are an integral part of any Indian meal. Whether they are served in Baltistan or in the Balti Houses in Pakistan, is irrelevant. The fact is, they add that extra zest to spicy meals and make the entire meal much more interesting.

Traditionally, mild, creamy yogurt is used for raitas. Whole milk natural set yogurts are ideal as is Greek yogurt.

Yogurt is excellent for fighting bacteria related to gastro-intestinal problems. It is wholesome, versatile and very easy to digest.

Ghia ki Chutney

(Courgette Chutney)

Serves 4–6

The combination of courgette and coconut is wonderful. Traditionally, tender marrow is used in this chutney.

50g/2oz desiccated coconut
225g/8oz courgettes, roughly chopped
300ml/½ pint water
½ teaspoon salt or to taste
1 teaspoon tamarind concentrate or 1 tablespoon lime juice
1 green chilli, seeded and chopped
1cm/½ inch cube root ginger, peeled and roughly chopped
1 small clove garlic, peeled
15g/½oz coriander leaves, including tender stalks

1. Put the coconut, courgettes and water in a karahi, wok or saucepan and place over high heat. Bring to the boil, reduce the heat to low, cover and simmer for 5 minutes. Add the salt and tamarind, and stir until the tamarind is dissolved. Remove from the heat and allow to cool.

2. Purée the courgette mixture with the remaining ingredi
   ents in a food processor until smooth. If using lime juice,
   add this while blending.

Preparation time: 5 minutes

Cooking time: 6–8 minutes

Serving ideas: Serve with Shakahari Shamee Kabab
   (pages 36–7), Shakurkandi Pakoras (pages 51–3) or Palak
   Pakoras (pages 47–8).

Suitable for freezing.

Ghia ka Raita

(Courgette Raita)

Serves 4

Raitas, pickles and chutneys make Indian meals more appetizing. Raitas are very easy to make and any vegetable can be used for them. I love courgettes or tender marrow stir-fried with garlic before mixing with natural yogurt. I have flavoured this raita with roasted cumin seeds.

1 teaspoon cumin seeds
½ teaspoon black peppercorns
1 tablespoon sunflower or corn oil
2 small or 1 large clove garlic, peeled and crushed
225g/8oz courgettes, cut into bite-sized pieces
½ teaspoon salt or to taste
150g/5oz thick set whole milk natural yogurt

1. Preheat a cast-iron griddle or a heavy-based frying pan over medium heat. When hot, dry roast the cumin seeds and peppercorns for 1–2 minutes or until the spices release their aroma. Remove from the pan and allow to cool thoroughly, then crush with a mortar and pestle.

2. Preheat a karahi or wok over medium heat for 1–2

minutes, then add the oil. When hot but not smoking, stir-fry the garlic until lightly browned.

3. Add the courgettes and salt and stir-fry for 2 minutes. Remove from the heat and allow to cool thoroughly.
4. Put the yogurt in a medium mixing bowl and beat with a fork until smooth. Add the courgettes and half the crushed spices. Chill until required. Serve sprinkled with remaining crushed spices.

Preparation time: 10 minutes
Cooking time: 5–6 minutes
Serving ideas: Serve with any Balti meal.

Mooli aur Gajjar Ka Raita

(Radish and Carrot Raita)

Serves 4–6

Mooli (white radish) is becoming increasingly available in supermarkets. Combined with carrots, it makes a lovely relish.

100g/4oz thick set whole milk natural yogurt
1 teaspoon salt or to taste
1 teaspoon sugar
1 teaspoon bottled mint sauce
½ red onion (about 50g/2oz), finely chopped
1 mooli (about 225g/8oz), grated
2 carrots (about 200g/7oz) grated

1. Beat the yogurt with a fork until smooth. Add the salt, sugar, mint and onion and mix thoroughly.
2. Stir in the grated mooli and carrots, mix and chill.

Preparation time: 15 minutes
Cooking time: Nil
Serving ideas: Serve with any Balti meal accompanied by naan or rice.

Variation: Use white cabbage instead of mooli.

188

Tamatar aur Khira ka Raita

(Tomato and Cucumber Raita)

Serves 4–6

Raita is an important part of an Indian meal and it is enjoyed by vegetarians and meat eaters alike. Plain yogurt, seasoned in a variety of ways, is the basis of any raita. Yogurt has been consumed in India from ancient times. Besides being whole-some and versatile, it is also easy on the digestive system.

150g/5oz thick set whole milk natural yogurt
½ teaspoon salt
1 teaspoon sugar
2 firm ripe tomatoes (about 150g/5oz), seeded and chopped
small piece of cucumber (about 150g/5oz), chopped
2 tablespoons finely chopped red onion
1 tablespoon finely chopped coriander leaves
2 teaspoons sunflower or corn oil
½ teaspoon black mustard seeds
6–8 curry leaves

1. Put the yogurt in a mixing bowl and add the salt and sugar. Beat until smooth.

189

2. Add the tomatoes, cucumber, onion and coriander leaves and mix thoroughly.

3. Preheat a karahi or wok over medium heat for 1–2 minutes and add the oil. When hot but not smoking, add the mustard seeds and curry leaves. As soon as the mustard seeds pop, remove the pan from heat and pour the entire contents over the Raita. Stir and mix, chill before serving.

Preparation time: 15 minutes
Cooking time: 2–3 minutes
Serving ideas: Serve with any Balti meal.

Pudina aur Hara Dhaniya ki Chutney

(Mint and Coriander Dip)

Serves 4–6

Mint is used extensively in Balti dishes. Kashmir, which is well known for karahi (Balti) cooking, has lovely floating gardens where mint is grown in abundance. If you cannot find fresh mint use bottled mint sauce and omit the lime juice.

15g/½oz mint
15g/½oz coriander leaves
1 tablespoon coarsely chopped red onion
1 green chilli, seeded and chopped
2 small cloves garlic, peeled and chopped
½ teaspoon salt
1 teaspoon sugar
100g/4oz thick set whole milk natural yogurt
25g/1oz ground almonds
1 tablespoon lime juice

1. Remove the mature stalks from the mint and coriander. Leave the tender ones on, wash and chop them roughly.

191

2. Put all the ingredients into a blender and purée until smooth. Chill for 2–3 hours before serving.

Preparation time: 10 minutes

Cooking time: Nil

Serving ideas: Serve with any deep-fried dishes and/or grilled or fried pappodums.

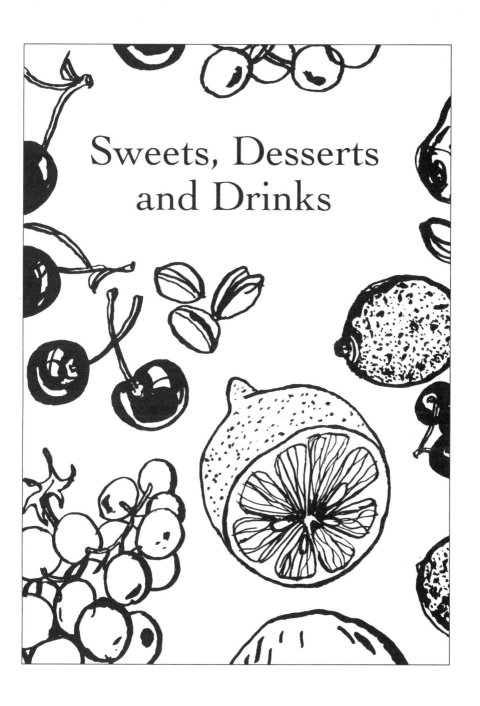

Sweets, Desserts and Drinks

Many recipes in this section consists of those served in traditional Balti/Karahi eateries in northern Pakistan and northern India.

I have used fruits and other ingredients characteristic of these regions to create some new recipes. The dairy products used in these recipes will provide you with plenty of protein and essential minerals. The majority of these dishes are straightforward and simple.

Gulab Jamoon

(Dried Milk Balls in Syrup)

Makes 16

A well-known and much loved sweetmeat from Northern India, Gulab Jamoon is traditionally made with 'khoya' and 'chenna'. Both of these are dairy products which can be made at home, but khoya is quite time consuming. An easy alternative is to use full cream dried milk powder which you can buy from Asian shops. I have simplified it further by using dried skimmed milk powder which is easily obtainable, and to make up the richness, added single cream to the dried milk. The jamoons are cooked twice — first in hot oil and then, immediately, in boiling sugar syrup. This operation needs to be carried out simultaneously, but don't worry it is not as bad as it may sound! Serve the jamoons at room temperature with tea or coffee or chilled with a little whipped cream as a dessert.

175g/6oz dried skimmed milk powder
75g/3oz fine semolina
1 teaspoon ground cardamom
1 teaspoon baking powder
40g/1½oz ghee or unsalted butter, melted
150ml/¼ pint single cream

25g/1oz shelled unsalted pistachio nuts, chopped
350g/12oz granulated sugar
900ml/1½ pints water
Oil for deep frying
2 tablespoons rose water

1. Put the milk powder, semolina, ground cardamom and baking powder in a large mixing bowl and mix thoroughly. Add the ghee or butter and rub in until blended thoroughly.

2. Add the cream and mix until a soft dough is formed. Knead the dough on a pastry board until smooth. Divide the dough into 2 equal parts and make 8 equal-sized balls from each. Stuff each ball with chopped pistachio nuts and make them as smooth and round as possible without any surface cracks. You can do this by rotating them between your palms.

3. Heat the oil in a karahi or wok over medium heat. At the same time, put the sugar and water in a karahi, wok or saucepan and bring to the boil. Stir until the sugar has dissolved. Turn the heat down to medium-low and simmer while you fry the jamoons.

4. Deep-fry the jamoons in batches in a single layer until they are a rich dark brown colour. When you first put them in the hot oil, they will sink. After 2–3 minutes they will start floating in the oil, if they do not, gently ease them away from the base of the pan using a thin spatula. Turn over once or twice until brown, then remove with a slotted spoon and put straight into the simmering syrup.

Cook for 1 minute in the syrup, then transfer to a glass bowl with a slotted spoon. Use 2 glass bowls and put 8 jamoons in each bowl. If you pile them up, they tend to lose their shape.

5. When you have cooked all the jamoons, add the rose water to the remaining syrup. Spoon the rose-flavoured syrup over the jamoons, dividing it equally between the bowls. Let them soak in the syrup for 30 minutes before serving.

Preparation time: 30 minutes
Cooking time: 15–20 minutes

Kesari Annanas

(Saffron-flavoured Pineapple)

Serves 6

Pineapples came to India from South America and in the early days they were found only in the areas near Baltistan. Today pineapple is a very popular fruit all over India. I have flavoured this lovely fruit with saffron and cinnamon. It makes a wonderfully refreshing way to finish a Balti meal.

>1 medium pineapple or 2 x 350g/12oz cans pineapple in
> syrup
>600ml/1 pint water
>100g/4 oz caster sugar
>3 x 2.5cm/1 inch pieces cassia bark or cinnamon sticks
>½ teaspoon saffron strands, pounded
>2 teaspoons ground arrowroot
>275g/10oz unflavoured fromage frais or whipped double
> cream
>375g/13oz can guava halves, drained

1. Skin the pineapple and remove the 'eyes' with a small sharp knife. Cut across into 12 slices and remove the hard core with an apple corer. If using canned pineapple, drain

199

and reserve the syrup.

2. Put the water, sugar and cassia or cinnamon in a large saucepan 'and place over a high heat. Bring to the boil, then add the pineapple rings. Cook for 8–10 minutes, and transfer to a large plate with a slotted spoon.

3. Return the saucepan to the heat and add the saffron. Bring to the boil, reduce the heat to medium and cook for 6–7 minutes or until the syrup has reduced to nearly half its original volume. If using canned pineapple, measure 425ml/14 fl oz of the syrup and place over high heat. Add the cassia or cinnamon and bring to the boil. Reduce the heat to low and simmer for 5–6 minutes. Add the saffron and simmer for 6–8 minutes. Strain the syrup, return to the saucepan and place over a medium heat. When it begins to bubble, blend the arrowroot with a little water and add to the syrup, stirring. Cook for 2–3 minutes when the syrup will thicken slightly. Remove from the heat and allow to cool.

4. Stack 2 pineapple rings together and place in an individual serving dish. Fill the hollow with fromage frais or cream, spreading about 1 tablespoon on the top but leaving a thin border of pineapple showing. Carefully remove the seeds from guava halves with a teaspoon, then place the guavas on the fromage or cream, hollow side down.

5. Pour on enough saffron-flavoured syrup to cover the pineapple, but not the fromage frais, and chill until required.

Preparation time: 10–25 minutes

Cooking time: 15–20 minutes

Gajjar ka Halwa

(Carrot Fudge)

Serves 4–6

Gajjarka Halwa is a very popular dessert in the northern territories of India and Pakistan. It is made by simmering grated carrots with milk and sugar with a hint of spices. Dried fruits and nuts are also added and I have selected those characteristic of Baltistan and other Himalayan regions.

> 600ml/1 pint full cream milk
> 400g/14oz carrots, scraped and finely grated
> 100g/4oz caster sugar
> 40g/1½oz ghee
> 25g/1oz almonds, blanched and slivered
> 25g/1oz shelled walnut, broken into bite-sized pieces
> 25g/1oz seedless raisins
> ½ teaspoon ground cardamom
> ½ teaspoon ground nutmeg
> 2 tablespoons double cream
> Whipped double cream to serve

1. Put the milk and carrots in a karahi or wok and bring to the boil over high heat. Reduce the heat to medium, then cook for 15–20 minutes or until the milk evaporates com-

pletely. Stir regularly, scraping up and mixing in any thickened milk that sticks to the sides of the pan. If you do not do this, the milk that is stuck will burn, giving the dessert an unpleasant flavour.

2. Add the sugar and cook, stirring constantly, until the mixture is dry again. Remove from the heat and set aside. If you do not have another karahi, transfer the carrot mixture to a plate. Clean the karahi, place over medium heat and add the ghee. When hot but not smoking, stir-fry the almonds and walnuts until golden brown. Remove with a slotted spoon and drain on absorbent paper.

3. Fry the raisins until they swell up, then drain on absorbent paper. Stir the cardamom and nutmeg into the remaining ghee and immediately follow with the cooked carrot mixture. Stir-fry for 2–3 minutes, then blend in the cream. Reserving a few nuts and raisins, stir the remainder into the carrots. Remove from the heat and transfer to a serving dish. Garnish with the reserved nuts and raisins. Serve hot or cold with a little whipped cream.

Preparation time: 20 minutes
Cooking time: 40–45 minutes

Aam ki Kulfi

(Iced Mango Dessert)

Serves 8

Kulfi is the best known and most popular iced dessert in India. The name 'kulfi' is derived from the conical shaped metal moulds in which it is frozen. Opinions vary as to the origin of kulfi, some believe that it was brought to India by the mighty Moguls from Kabul. Others say that it originated in India after the arrival of the Moguls.

Traditional kulfi moulds are available in some Asian shops, but you can use small plastic containers or decorative individual jelly moulds instead. To give you an idea of the size, traditional moulds hold about two tablespoons of kulfi mix. I often set them in ice lolly moulds too.

375g/13oz can evaporated milk
300ml/½ pint single cream
1½ tablespoons ground rice
100g/4oz granulated sugar
1 teaspoon ground cardamom
450g/1lb mango purée
25g/1oz shelled unsalted pistachio nuts, roasted and lightly crushed

1. Mix the evaporated milk and single cream together in

203

a heavy-based saucepan and place over medium heat.

2. Mix together the ground rice and sugar, then sprinkle onto the milk mixture, stirring.

3. Continue to stir and cook until the mixture has thickened slightly, this will take 6–8 minutes.

4. Add the ground cardamom, stir and mix thoroughly, and remove from the heat. Allow to cool completely, keeping an eye on the mixture and stirring now and again to prevent a skin forming. When completely cold, stir in the mango purée.

5. Fill small containers of your choice with the mix and put in the freezer for 4–5 hours. Leave at room temperature for 5–6 minutes before removing from the moulds. The texture of kulfi is much harder than that of conventional ice cream.

6. Serve sprinkled with roasted pistachio nuts.

Preparation time: 5 minutes, plus freezing
Cooking time: 10 minutes

Papita aur Anar ki Mithai

(Papaya and Pomegranate Dessert)

Serves 4

The papaya (pawpaw) tree is a common sight in most gardens in the eastern foothills of the Himalayas. I have grown up eating fresh papayas brought down from the tree, they are sweet and juicy, and have a richer reddish pink colour than the ones we see in the shops today. Make sure the papaya is fully ripe before you try this recipe. When ripe, the skin has a yellow tinge and feels slightly soft to the touch. If they feel hard, leave them at room temperature for a couple of days and they will be just right. Pomegranate is sold by good supermarkets. It is excellent for adding that exotic touch, it is the seeds that are eaten and these have to be removed carefully from the fruit.

> 2 ripe papaya
> 1 pomegranate
> 225g/8oz unflavoured fromage frais or whipped double
>   cream
> 1 tablespoon rose water
> few mint leaves to decorate

1. Trim both ends of the papaya and cut in half lengthwise. Carefully ease away the seeds with a teaspoon and scrape off the white membrane.
2. Cut the pomegranate in half lengthwise, remove the seeds with a fork, and reserve. If it is really fresh and ripe, you can peel the outer skin like an orange. Remove the white membrane and pith.
3. Mix the fromage frais or cream with the rose water.
4. Line individual serving dishes with some of the reserved pomegranate seeds and place a papaya half in the centre. Fill the hollows with fromage frais or cream. Top with the remaining pomegranate seeds and decorate with mint leaves. Chill for 2–3 hours.

Preparation time: 15–20 minutes
Cooking time: Nil

Phirni

(Ground Rice and Milk Dessert)

Serves 4

This delicious dessert with dried fruits and nuts is flavoured with saffron and rose water with a hint of spices. Traditionally it is chilled and served in earthenware bowls. The addition of evaporated milk is not traditional, but I use it to speed up the cooking process.

> ½ teaspoon saffron strands, pounded
> 2 tablespoons very hot milk
> 15g/½oz ghee
> 40g/1½oz ground rice
> 25g/1oz raw cashews, split
> 25g/1oz seedless raisins
> 600ml/1 pint milk
> 300ml/½ pint evaporated milk
> 50g/2oz caster sugar
> ½ teaspoon ground cardamom
> ½ teaspoon ground nutmeg
> 1 tablespoon rose water
> 50g/2oz dried ready-to-eat apricots, sliced

207

25g/1oz walnut pieces, lightly browned in a little ghee or
butter

15g/½oz shelled unsalted pistachio nuts, lightly crushed
and browned as for walnuts

1. Soak the saffron strands in the hot milk and set aside.
2. Melt the ghee over a low heat in a karahi, wok or heavy-based saucepan, and add the ground rice, cashews and raisins. Stir-fry for 1 minute and add the milk. Increase the heat to high, stir until smoke rises, then reduce the heat and cook for 10–12 minutes or until the mixture thickens slightly, stirring constantly.
3. Add the evaporated milk and sugar, and continue to stir and cook until the mixture resembles the consistency of pouring custard.
4. Add the saffron milk, ground cardamom and nutmeg, stir and cook for 1 minute.
5. Add the rose water, stir and remove from the heat. Stir in half the apricots and allow to cool thoroughly. Stir frequently to prevent a skin forming.
6. Transfer the mixture to a serving dish and chill for 3–4 hours. Top with the remaining apricots and the fried nuts.

Preparation time: 10 minutes
Cooking time: 30–35 minutes

Phalon ka Chaat

V

(Spiced Fruit Salad)

Serves 4

This is a fabulous combination of exotic fruits which is delicately spiced. Serve it with a cup of Masala Chai (see pages 214–15) for a perfect end to your meal.

2 ripe pomegranates
1 large ripe papaya
1 small or ½ medium pineapple
175g/6oz seedless green grapes
175g/6oz seedless black grapes
½ teaspoon ground dry ginger
¼ teaspoon freshly milled black pepper
½ teaspoon ground cumin
Pinch of chilli powder
¼ teaspoon dried mint or 6–8 fresh mint leaves, finely
    chopped
½ teaspoon salt

1. Cut the pomegranates into halves and remove the seeds by peeling off the outer skin like you would peel an orange. If you find this difficult to do, gently ease away

209

the seeds with a fork and discard the outer skin. Remove white membrane and skin next to the seeds and reserve the seeds.

2. Cut the papaya into half lengthwise and remove the black seeds, scrape off the white membrane you will find under the seeds. Cut the papaya into 2.5cm/1 inch cubes.

3. Peel the pineapple and remove the 'eyes' with a small sharp knife. Remove the central hard core and cut the pineapple into bite sized pieces.

4. Halve the grapes and mix all the prepared fruits in a large mixing bowl. Add the remaining ingredients, except the salt, and mix thoroughly. Chill for 1–2 hours. Stir in the salt and serve.

Preparation time: 25–30 minutes

Cooking time: Nil

Variation: Use a fresh, ripe mango instead of papaya and fresh lychees instead of grapes.

Meethi Lassi

(Sweet Lassi)

Makes 1.1 litres/2 pints

Lassi, sweet or savoury, is a well known and popular drink all over Northern India where the climate can be extreme. The bitter winter is followed by a blazing summer when Lassi is drunk for a cooling effect, on its own or with meals.

450g/1lb thick set whole milk natural yogurt
600ml/1 pint water
65g/2½oz caster sugar
1 tablespoon rose water
Crushed ice to serve

1. Put all the ingredients except the ice in a blender and blend thoroughly. If you do not have a blender, beat the yogurt until smooth and gradually add the water. Continue to beat until well blended. Add the sugar and rose water and stir until the sugar is dissolved.
2. Pour into tall glasses lined with crushed ice.

Preparation time: A few minutes

Namkeen Lassi

(Savoury Lassi)

Makes 1.1 litres/2 pints

Savoury Lassi, with a touch of spices, served in tall glasses lined with crushed ice, is indeed a welcome sight during the oppressive Indian summer months. Serve any time as a refreshing drink or with meals.

½ teaspoon cumin seeds
½ teaspoon black peppercorns
4500g/1lb thick set whole milk natural yogurt
12–14 mint leaves
1½ teaspoon salt or to taste
2 teaspoons sugar
600ml/1 pint water
Crushed ice to serve

1. Preheat a karahi or other small heavy-based pan over medium heat. Add the cumin and peppercorns, stir and roast until they release their aroma. This will only take a minute or two. Remove from the pan and allow to cool, then crush with a mortar and pestle.

2. Put the crushed spices in a blender and add the yogurt,

mint, salt, sugar and half the water. Blend until the mint and spices are thoroughly incorporated. Mix in the remaining water, then pour into tall glasses lined with crushed ice.

Masala Chai

(Spiced Tea)

Serves 4

Masala Chai is very popular in the cold, hilly terrain of India, especially during the winter months. An infusion is made by boiling water and winter spices such as cardamom, cinnamon and cloves and the tea is brewed in this. These spices are known to create body heat and this is another way to keep warm in the bitter climate. Serve Masala Chai after dinner or at any other time as a warming drink.

750ml/1¼ pints water
1 x 5cm/2 inch piece cassia bark or cinnamon stick
6 green cardamom pods, split to the top of each pod
4 whole cloves
½ teaspoon fennel seeds
4 teaspoons Assam or Darjeeling leaf tea
Milk and sugar to taste

1. Put the water, cassia or cinnamon, cardamom, cloves and fennel in a saucepan and bring to the boil. Reduce the heat to low, cover and simmer for 5 minutes.

2. Rinse out a teapot with boiling water and add the tea

214

leaves. Strain the spiced liquid into the teapot and brew for 4–5 minutes.

3. Put milk and sugar to taste in individual cups and strain the tea over.

☙ Index